Black Widow Betty Neumar

Erica Newton

Published by Trellis Publishing, 2021.

BLACK WIDOW BETTY NEUMAR

First edition. July 5, 2021.

ISBN: 979-8224181308

Written by Erica Newton.

BLACK WIDOW BETTY

ERICA NEWTON

The Black Widow Betty Neumar

ERICA NEWTON

There's usually a certain characteristic or gender we think of when we hear the word "serial-killer," but in the case of Betty Neumar, everything changed. Most times, serial-killers are either caught or found dead before they reach senior status, but in this case, the opposite is true.

Investigators spoke of Betty's world becoming "a nation-wide web of coincidences." Because of this figurative web, the media dubbed her the Black Widow. In all her 79 years on this planet, she had been married five times, and each of her relationships had ended with an unexpected death of her husband.

To the outside world, family members who are unconvinced of Betty's involvement in the murders and deaths of her husbands call her a "Bee – a friendly woman who operated beauty shops, attended church, and raised money for charity." Other family members saw a different side of Betty; an uglier side of fist fights at family gatherings, use of vulgar language and demeaning relatives, her two-faced personality where she would put on a show for the public eye, and her notoriety for being an exceedingly greedy woman whose only ambitions in live revolved around having and spending as much money as possible.

On June 30, 2011, the Black Widow, died while under police custody. She was currently at a local hospital for treating her cancer which ultimately took her life. Unfortunately for the relatives of the murdered men and police investigators who have been following Betty closely in search of any slip-up or record of her shady past, her passing away meant that she was exonerated of any and all charges made against her. The public was understandingly disappointed with the final verdict but nothing could be done to overturn the law.

The world will forever know Betty Nebular as the Black Widow who did away with at least four of her husbands. Betty Neumar, who would later be called the Black Widow by the media, was born in 1931. She was raised in an underprivileged home in a coal mining community. Terry Sanders, Betty's son-in-law who has been married to one of her daughters for more than 35 years, told reporters that Betty "was a tough country girl and fought through a lot of pain."

In November 1950, then-18-year-old Betty Johnson, a daughter of a coal miner in Ironton, Ohio, married a local boy named Clarence Malone. The marriage didn't last long due to her filing a report to Ironton police about Clarence physically abusing her. Although they produced a son together, Betty and Clarence separated from each other. They virtually had no contact with each other from after their divorce up until his unexpected death nearly 20 years later.

In 1953, Betty married James F. Flynn, a New Yorker notorious for his bad drinking habits. Their marriage didn't last long when in 1955 he was found dead. Betty told contradicting stories of her second husband's death over the following years. She reported that he died in a car accident, was killed on a pier in New York City, and died from hypothermia in the snow. To date, the exact cause and circumstances behind James' death remain unknown.

While working in Jacksonville, Florida, in 1964, Betty married a 29-year-old man from the Navy named Richard Sills. Only three years later, the police had discovered the dead body of Richard with an apparent gunshot wound in the couple's bedroom of their mobile home in Big Coppitt Key, Florida. Betty had told police investigators that her late husband had pulled out a .22-caliber pistol in the heat of an argument.

For some reason during their scuffle, he turned the gun onto himself and pulled the trigger, shooting himself in the heart. Without an autopsy to confirm or deny this claim, his death was ruled a suicide by the police. Richard's death was officially ruled a suicide by law authorities, but in 2008, after her arrest, medical examiner reports emerged that showed Richard had been shot twice.

Finding two gunshot wounds in a suicide victim was odd but unfortunately could not be used as a lead to convicting Betty. Monroe County officials denied requests to exhume Sills' body or take investigative action in light of this new piece of evidence because the statute of limitations had already expired.

Investigators from the Naval Criminal Investigative Services found the case of Sills' highly skeptical and had plans to investigate as soon as Betty's case in North Carolina was completed. However, as of 2011, the NCI spokesperson Ed Buice who mentioned previously of their intentions to investigate had told the public that after Betty's death the NCIS would no longer pursue her case.

One of Richard's sons from a previous marriage, Michael Sills, expressed his massive disappointment with the NCIS's decision to halt investigations, but he became enraged at officials from Florida for their failure in providing closure on his father's death. He had never gotten the chance to know his father since his parents had divorced only when he was a toddler and his mother gained custody rights.

"As far as I'm concerned, she did it," Michael said in an interview. "There's too many inconsistent things about it." He further went on to state that his late father's military files paint him as a man who was not depressed nor did he have suicidal tendencies.

Betty would then go on to marry a man in the army named Harold Gentry in January 1968. Only two years into her marriage with Harold, the body of Clarence – Betty's first husband who separated from her in 1952 – was found outside of his automobile repair shop in a town near Cleveland, Ohio with a bullet hole in his head. Police investigators never identified the gunman who had shot him execution-style in the back of his head.

One of Clarence's brothers told newspaper reporters that he did not suspect Betty as being involved in their late brother's murder case since they had been separated for more than 15 years and she had remarried twice since then. In fact, there were rumors that Clarence had gotten into trouble with a local motorcycle gang who could have potentially murdered him.

In 1985, Betty's eldest son, Gary Flynn who was adopted by Betty's second husband and took his last name, was also found shot to death in his apartment complex in the Cleveland area. Betty was named the beneficiary of Gary's life insurance policy so she received a check worth $10,000 after his death. Once again, the police were stumped by the case and never officially identified who his killer was.

Some of James' family members were highly skeptical that he would commit suicide, despite there being a suicide note. Their suspicions grew when they learned that Betty would be receiving a $10,000 life insurance check following James' death. Jeff Carstensen, a stepson of Gary, told investigators about memories of their ugly holiday gatherings fueled by excessive alcohol consumption. "Gary Flynn may have had his own demons," Jeff said in an interviewer. At the time of Richard's (the third husband) death, Gary and Peggy (one of Betty's daughters from a previous marriage) were in the next room when Richard was fatally shot.

Jeff spoke of his stepfather's paranoia about banks when he was interrogated by police investigators. Gary considered himself a survivalist that would sometimes go on the occasional drug and alcohol binges after speaking with Betty on the phone. Jeff told detectives that he and his mother, Cecelia Flynn, raced to Gary's home from Michigan to get there before Betty. They suspected that Gary had a large amount of money hidden in a room he rented at the Perry Township duplex.

He told detectives that he and his mother had discovered upwards of $16,000 in cash hidden below Gary's bed. They also reported finding several guns and ammunition. Betty would arrive later to collect the ashes of her late son the day after his death.

Two years later, Jeff, a newly-divorced man, moved to Georgia to live with Betty. Not long after, he returned to Michigan after he discovered that Betty had gotten him fired from two jobs. Betty also played a role in ruining the relationship between him and his girlfriend at the time.

Betty made the relationship between Jeff and herself even worse when she offered to take out a $100,000 life insurance policy on him and name herself as the beneficiary. "I got out of there as soon as I could," Jeff said. "She told me that people of our stature have insurance policies on each other. That way, if something happens to you, you take care of me, and if something happens to me, I take care of you. It was all too suspicious. So I got out of there any way I could." He would later learn that anybody who was even remotely involved in Betty's life would have something bad happen to them.

In July 1968, Betty and Harold, who was now retired from the army, resided in Norwood, North Carolina. After 18 years of having a less-than-harmonious marriage, a reported six bullets were fired into the body of Harold. Betty told investigators that she had been out of town when her fourth husband was riddled with bullets in his own home. Again, the police were unable to name a suspect in this shooting. However, due to Harold's sudden death, Betty again received a life insurance policy check worth $50,000.

"Over the years [during their marriage]," Al Gentry – brother to Harold – told reporters, "She told our family that she had been a nurse and that her first husband died of cancer. She also said she was a beautician and lived in Ohio, and had children from a previous marriage." During their time together, Harold worked long hours as a delivery truck driver for the Royal Chemical Co., while Betty worked in a drug store, drove school buses, and even waited tables in local restaurants.

When the police reopened the case after listening to Al's pleas and suspicion of Betty, there were several delays. The first delay which virtually let Betty free from trial occurred in 1986 when the files with the police investigators were given to prosecutors. Betty's trial was set and supposed to start on February 26 of that year, but it was ultimately postponed in order to give the newly elected prosecutor more time to prepare his case. Al, frustrated with the postpone, told reporters, "We still haven't answered the question: Who actually killed my brother?"

From the beginning of the initial investigation, law enforcement officials told the public that they had trouble in piecing together the details of Betty's life due to inconsistencies and alterations made in her retellings. However, through winding interviews, documents, and court records, a general outline of her history could be deduced based on the existing records of her life in North Carolina, Ohio, Florida, and Georgia (the states where she officially wedded her five husbands).

In 1991, the then-60-year-old widow/serial killer married her fifth and last husband named John Neumar. After nine years of marriage, the couple managed to owe a collective $200,000 on 43 different credit cards and soon filed for bankruptcy. In October 2007, John died at age 79. His official ruling of death was listed as sepsis – a blood infection caused by bacterial exposure. However, John's children hold onto different beliefs of whether Betty played a role in poisoning him with arsenic.

John K. Neumar, son of John Neumar, Sr., told reporters that he didn't suspect Betty of slipping arsenic or another toxic substance into John, Sr.'s food or drink. However, he doubted whether Betty could truly be called innocent. "She was a user," John, Jr. told reporters when asked about Betty as a person. Janet Neumar, one of the daughters, spoke of her father being a "picture of health. He [never had a] sick day in his life until he wound up marrying Betty." She believes that Betty was actively involved in poisoning her father.

John K. Neumar had a number of questions regarding his stepmother, Betty, and her possible involvement in his father's death. The charge against Betty had nothing to do with his father's death, but he felt that due to her past she was most likely involved in some way with slipping poison into his father's drink. As soon as he heard news of her arrest, his own thoughts returned to his father who had died only the previous year.

"He passed away recently," John told reporters while speaking of his late father, "and when he passed she never called me and told me he was sick or nothing. And when I found out he wa dead I read about it in the paper. And before I could go see him, he was cremated."

When Betty was arrested, John, Jr. wasn't even slightly surprised. "With the relationship I had with her over the years, and the way she pulled my father away from me, I mean, nothing shocked me." He spoke of not having a communicative relationship with his father for several years prior to his death. "From the time my father married her, it didn't take long for a split to grow between our families. And it just got wider as the years got older."

Strangely, although John had a burial plot prepared for his body after death, Betty wanted her husband's body to be cremated as quickly as possible. Those who suspect Betty of murdering John often talk about how suspicious she was in wanting him cremated, and even claim it was done in order to avoid an autopsy where a toxicology test would show his real cause of death.

"Makes me wonder now why he got cremated so quick and nobody told me he was sick or died 'til he was cremated," John, Jr. told reporters. "I want to know why he was cremated before I even [knew] he was dead. This leads me to ask that question." The Stanly County Sheriff said this was a dead case that was recently resurrected after they received an anonymous tip regarding Betty's contacting a hired killer.

After two long decades of pleading with the police to investigate Betty after Harold's death, his brother Al convinced police investigators to take another look at his case. At the time there were still no suspects named in the killing of Harold, but there was large suspicion surrounding Betty. When the police finally listened to what Al had been saying, they finally arrested Betty who was 76 years old at the time. She was charged with hiring an assassin to gun Harold down. "She [was] 76 years old," lead detective Williams told reporters right after Betty's arrest. "She does not work. In fact, she was working in her garden when the detectives came and spoke to her."

"This is something I've been waiting for for a long time," Al told reporters in 2008. If it hadn't been for Al's persistence in communicating his worries and suspicions to the police investigators, they probably wouldn't have been able to link Betty to the deaths of her previous husbands.

After her arrest, they soon discovered that she had been married for a total of five times, and each of those marriages ended with each of her husbands either succumbing to gunshots or a suspicious illness. Authorities had notified the law officials where Betty was last known to have lived with each of her husbands. At the time, none of their deaths were even considered suspicious, but they ended up reopening some of the cold cases.

Al had always suspected Betty of murdering his brother in their home on July 14, 1988. Al told any police investigator who would listen that although Betty was out of town at the time of Harold's death, she had "shown no emotion when she got back."

Police records show that as soon as she had arrived at her one-story house in a quiet, peaceful neighborhood, she and her house were surrounded by flashing lights and several policemen. As soon as she was approached, she blurted out that she had been in Augusta, Georgia, the previous night, even before the police could get a word out.

Al's suspicion of his sister-in-law increased by her steely cold behavior after the sudden murder of her husband at the time. "No tears," he began as he told his suspicions of his sister-in-law to police investigators and reporters. "If she had gotten out of the car with tears in her eyes and asked me why would anybody kill Harold, I would have never suspected her at all," Al told reporters as he remembers that day he first saw Betty after his brother's death. "That's where she slipped up." Al told of her history together with Harold during their 18 years of marriage, "At first she was pleasant, but she grew to become cold to my brother and family. By 1986, the marriage was strained and Harold Gentry was living in a camper in the front yard."

Al recalls Betty being a person who was accustomed to living the good life with jewelry and clothes. "She had the means to live like that but that wasn't enough. She always wanted more, more, more. And she found a way to get it."

In 2008, after a homicide investigation done in North Carolina, a grand jury indicted Betty Neumar on three counts of solicitation to commit first-degree murder of her fourth husband, Harold Gentry. Investigators said that Betty had requested from three people – a former policeman, a neighbor, and a third person – to commit the murder of her then-husband. None of these three men accepted her request, but a fourth unidentified man did carry out the plot and fulfill the contract killing.

The then-76-year-old woman sitting in a North Carolina Jail was accused of hiring a contract killer to assassinate Harold Gentry. The authorities were also re-examining the cases of her other former husbands and their untimely deaths. No motive had been discussed, but records and interviews with Betty's relatives all point to her personality as a "domineering matriarch consumed by money" to be the main motive behind her alleged murder cases.

Al Gentry saw his sister-in-law for the first time after several years on the morning of her trial in North Carolina. He was recorded to make an off-the-cuff remark about her orange jumpsuit being "the prettiest outfit I've ever seen her in."

At the time of her arrest, she did not have an attorney. Her daughter with Harold, who lives in Augusta, Georgia, has declined to comment about the arrest of her mother and of her alleged involvement in the deaths of her previous husbands.

Rick Burris, the sheriff who reopened the mysterious case of Harold Gentry, was not the leading figure of his department during the time of Harold's death. Burris told reporters that he had reviewed the stacks of files and accessed transcripts of interviews conducted byt the State Bureau of Investigation. He also said that the reports pointed to the large possibility that Betty had hired a contract killer to take Harold out of the picture. However, at the time there was insufficient evidence to charge her and she was allowed to walk free.

Rick had assigned an investigator to re-examine the recorded evidence and hold interviews with all of the parties involved in this case. "She was a suspect for a long time but we didn't have enough evidence. Now we do," Burris told reporters shortly after Betty's arrest.

Scott Williams was assigned the task of finding out how Betty had done away with her fourth husband, Harold Gentry. The lead detective spoke of the possibility that someone who had previously been contacted by Betty to carry out the murder plot went straight to the authorities to voice his concern. Unfortunately, nobody in the police station at the time took the claim seriously, and Harold's death came shortly after that.

Subsequent to her arrest, Georgia police investigators reopened the case of the death of John Neumar who had supposedly died of sepsis. However, due to the prompt cremation of the body, investigators were unable to find any evidence that Betty was involved in any way.

Betty's two daughters from previous marriages, Kelly and Peggy, remain steadfast in their mother's innocence. "She has been a caring, loving mother, and she's a loving, caring grandmother," Peggy told reporters.

Judge Lisa Thacker who was in charge of the Black Widow's proceedings in North Carolina refused to lower the $500,000 bond. Prosecutors called Betty a "flight risk" and other jurisdictions were "ramping up their investigations into her past." Betty's defense lawyer, Charles Parnell, argued that his client and frail then-76-year-old grandmother was not a flight risk and the bond "is completely excessive. It's unheard of." The Assistant District Attorney at the time, Tim Rodgers, disclosed the information of her 28 aliases on different passports, driver licenses, and credit cards. Her bail was set at $300,000.

After nearly a year after her arrest, Betty paid her $300,000 bail. It's not entirely certain where she received that much money to pay the bail. She was released from jail and promptly moved to Louisiana. In 2009, a television documentary aired on the BBC in the United Kingdom, titled "Black Widow Granny."

Film-maker Normal Hull had conducted interviews with both Betty and relatives of her late husbands who claimed that she had put an end to their lives for her economic aspirations. When confronted with these accusations, Betty simply told the reporter, "I cannot control when somebody dies. That's God's work," and that her accusers were nuts. "Later on it's going to eat their heart out," Betty told Normal Hull during one of their interview sessions, "The hate and discontent that they are living in now will make them miserable... I got no insurance from the last one, no insurance from the third one. After Harold died I got $50,000. But as far as all this money and this stuff goes, there wasn't none."

Despite the obvious torment caused by the accusations and the negative exposure by the media, Betty said that she was prepared to forgive them. "If you're going to heaven you have to forgive. You don't have to forget, but you have to forgive."

Al says that the pain of losing his brother still visits him from time to time. After her arrest, Al went straight to his brother's gravesite where he delivered a brief, four-worded message: "Brother, we got her."

But unfortunately for the brothers and the numerous family members seeking closure over the deaths of Betty's five husbands, they would never get the chance to hit her will the full force of the law.

Betty Neuman died of complications during her bout with cancer in June 2011. She was being treated at a Fork Polk, Louisiana, hospital at the time of her death. The Black Widow passed away before the North Carolina Police Force could try her for Harold's untimely murder. In accordance with the law, because of her death before an official trial, she was presumed innocent. None of her family members from her husbands' families share the same opinion.

Authorities from Georgia closed the re-examination of Betty's fifth husband since there was no evidence that could be taken from his body and their main suspect had passed away. His family has criticized the conclusion to the case. Al, Harold's brother, had lingering questions about Betty's past and her involvement in each of her husbands' deaths. He had hoped that everything would be exposed at the trial. "She took those secrets to the grave," he said in an interview. "I'm numb. I wanted justice and we're not going to get it."

Al Gentry, the man who spend more than two decades on his pursuit of the truth of his brother's killer, died only two years after the Black Widow's untimely passing. He passed in 2013 of a heart attack without having any closure on his murdered brother's case.

BLACK WIDOW LYDA TRUEBLOOD

JESSI DILLARD

A true "black widow"

Death followed Lyda Trueblood everywhere she went. At first glance, it may have seemed that the young woman was facing a run of bad luck – but as the run continued, suspicions began to arise.

Northeast of Kansas City, in the small town of Keytesville, Missouri, a true "black widow" was born on October 16, 1892. Over the course of her life, Lyda Anna Mae Trueblood took on seven married names, and is most well-known as Lyda Southard. However, Idaho remembers her as Lady Bluebeard – the state's first female serial killer.

"She swept the men of her choice off their feet – courted them so persistently that they could not escape," said V. H. Ormsby, a deputy sheriff from Twin Falls, Idaho. Ormsby was one of the officers who arrested Trueblood in Honolulu for the death of her fourth husband.

By the age of 27, Trueblood had already killed six people, including her own daughter. However, she would only be convicted of one murder – the poisoning of her fourth husband, Edward Meyer, in 1921.

"The marital experiences of the one-time Missouri country town girl eclipses even those of fiction. Ten years ago, while still in her teens, she was attending Sunday school and enjoying the popularity that goes with being a village belle."

Described as "pudgy faced and plain of figure," Trueblood still caught the eye of Robert Dooley, whose family was close with Trueblood's. Some said Trueblood was the most popular girl at her high school, claiming she had an "indefinable something, a spark giving off a light that draws men, by physiological and chemical attraction."

"They wasn't so wealthy, just so-so," said Mrs. Larrabee Hanson, who lived near the Trueblood family. "But they were all church-going people, devout and clean-living. (Trueblood) went to church every Sunday without fail."

A magazine writer, Alan Jaffe, who detailed Trueblood's history for a profile in *Argosy* magazine in 1957, said men "hung around her like flies about a honey pot." In fact, when Trueblood finally left her childhood home and moved to Twin Falls, Robert Dooley followed – and the two were married there in 1912, when she was only 21.

A promise of the future

"They had a perfectly normal relationship," said Mychel Matthews with the Twin Falls County Historical Museum. "They appeared to be just like the rest of the residents around town."

With the security of their future family in mind, the newlyweds decided to take out an insurance policy on Robert and his brother, Edward. If either died, the survivor would inherit $1,000 – with an equal amount going to Trueblood. And by August 1915, the couple was $2,000 richer. Edward Dooley had fallen ill and had died after just a few days – typhoid, the doctors said.

"There was nothing suspicious about the death," Matthews said. "It was ruled as food poisoning or typhoid."

As Edward lay dying, Trueblood convinced her husband to revise his insurance policy – for the family's protection, she argued. A new policy was drafted for Robert and his wife, stating that if either died, the surviving spouse would receive $2,000.

Just one month later, Robert Dooley followed in his brother's footsteps – succumbing to typhoid in a similar fashion. Trueblood, however, had begun to build herself a substantial nest egg. Only six weeks after losing her husband, Trueblood's infant daughter, Laura

Marie, "drank from a contaminated well," according to reports – leaving the widow lonely and desperate for companionship.

Since accidental poisonings did occasionally occur in rural areas, and epidemics – particularly typhoid – were rampant during that time, the deaths of the Dooleys were only briefly investigated by authorities.

"Little children died all the time, at that period of history," Matthews said. "She probably got a lot of sympathy, 'oh, that poor woman. She's lost her daughter, her husband, all to this stomach flu.'"

Trueblood endured a brief but mandatory period of mourning after losing her family, but soon struck up a relationship with a waiter at her favorite Twin Falls restaurant. William McHaffie married Trueblood just two years after the loss of her first husband and only child, and the couple immediately sought an insurance policy for William. Trueblood was named as William's only beneficiary, to receive $5,000 if anything was to happen to him.

The couple moved to Hardin, Montana, and only a year after they married, William died of "influenza." According to his friends and customers, William had always been a robust, healthy man – and the speed and depth of his sudden illness shocked them.

"Lyda Trublood was very careful," said crime author Diane Fanning. "She waited until they actually got sick – then, it was easier to believe that they had died of an illness. Everybody thought it was something he ate that finally did him in, but all that it was, really, was Lyda Trueblood."

Unfortunately for Trueblood, however, William had failed to pay the second premium on his insurance policy, letting it lapse. Trueblood received nothing for her efforts. Days after her late husband's funeral, Trueblood sold all her property and disappeared.

Moving on

After relocating to Denver, Trueblood managed to ensnare another victim – a farm machinery salesman she had met during her previous marriage to William. In fact, William had told friends that after he'd come to their door in an attempt to make a sale, Trueblood had seemed "struck" by him – and neighbours reported that the happy couple had even started fighting more after that.

Trueblood married Harlan Lewis in March of 1919, and took him with her back to Montana. The couple settled in Billings, and only one month later, Harlan took out a $10,000 life insurance policy. According to Matthews, the larger policies are an indication that Trueblood was manipulating the men in order to receive greater payouts.

"(Trueblood) was motivated by one thing, and one thing only - greed," said former FBI profiler Candice Delong. "She wanted money."

By mid-July, just three months after the wedding, disaster had struck. After falling ill to a sudden case "ptomaine poisoning," Harlan left Trueblood a widow for the third time – and this time, the cheque came through. After cashing out the estate, Trueblood disappeared again. Instead of heading somewhere new, however, Trueblood decided to return to Idaho.

Under the name of Lyda McHaffie, Trueblood checked into the Rogerson Hotel in Twin Falls in May 1919, and found herself a job at the Grille Café on Main Avenue. Business at the café picked up immediately, reports claim, and the foreman of Ira Perrine's Blue Lake Ranch, Edward Meyer, started visiting the restaurant regularly.

"Folks couldn't help noticing that the air sort of shimmered when (Trueblood's) eyes met Ed's," wrote Jaffe in his profile. "And that the ham he got was thicker, the eggs sunnier than those served other patrons."

The very next month, Trueblood moved to Pocatello, Idaho, where she married Edward Meyer and settled on a ranch.

"She rigged herself out fit to kill, bought a long mink coat and a closed car. Everybody in town was talking about the way she ran around to dances," said Ormsby. "She talked around town that she wasn't in love with Ed, but she wanted a home, and she said that sometime she might learn to love him."

Although she had started going by the name "Anna McHaffie," Trueblood showed no other signs of leaving her past life behind her. She applied for an insurance policy in Edward's name the day after the wedding, in the amount of $10,000 – however, the policy was not approved, and reasons were never clarified. It's possible that insurance companies were beginning to wise up to the run of bad luck Trueblood had encountered.

Suspicious situation

Only two weeks after the couple had wed, on August 25, Edward took ill. Doctors at the hospital claimed he had an excellent chance of recovery, but he was dead by September 7.

"She didn't wait for him to get sick," said Matthews. "Maybe she grew impatient, and that was probably the mistake she made in all of this."

Trueblood's previous husbands had been fairly low-key, unlikely to attract attention despite the unbelievable series of coincidences that had resulted in their deaths – and Trueblood's subsequent insurance claims. Edward Meyer, however, was a different case. As a prominent figure in Twin Falls, Edward had dealings with many of the leading business and farm people in the region – including the Twin Falls county sheriff.

"The townsfolk weren't just satisfied," Ormsby said. "They started a lot of talk, and the insurance company held up payment on the policy. The matter got into politics and folks wanted to know what the candidates for sheriff would do about (Trueblood)."

When traces of arsenic were discovered during a routine post-mortem examination, detectives finally brought the widow in for questioning.

"The investigation was just getting underway when the woman disappeared," stated an article published in the New York Times on

May 13, 1921. "Detectives traced her to Los Angeles, and kept track of her while the bodies of the two (Dooleys), the infant daughter, and McHaffie were exhumed and portions of the viscera were sent to chemists."

Edward Meyer's death had become somewhat of a political issue in the 1920 campaign for sheriff, and potential candidates were asked how they planned to handle the case. The current sheriff passed the case to a "remarkable" deputy, Virgin Ormsby – and the investigation would be virtually his only assignment for months.

"After she left for California, the town got more dissatisfied than ever, and in January, I was assigned to the case," Ormsby said. "I've had the bodies of the men dissatisfied and examined – three chemists each working separately reported to me that they found arsenic. I interviewed the doctors who attended the husbands and obtained statements from them that enabled me to build a strong case against her."

Ormsby even discovered that a relative of Trueblood's first husband and brother-in-law had been studying the suspicious deaths in his family. A chemist named Earl Dooley had already begun to consider the possibility that Robert and Edward Dooley had been poisoned with arsenic – and according to Fanning, his suspicions led him to investigate the scene of Trueblood's most recent victim.

After taking samples from Edward Meyer's vomit in the sand, Earl had them tested.

"Sure enough, he found arsenic – and when that happened, he went to a doctor to get it confirmed in another lab," Fanning said. "It was definitely arsenic."

Mounting evidence

Police first determined that the Dooley brothers had been poisoned, as well as Trueblood's own child. Officers in Montana started investigating the cases of Harlan Lewis and William McHaffie, intrigued by the seemingly impossible coincidences that had led

Trueblood to make so many insurance claims. Trueblood, meanwhile, was busy seducing her fifth husband, Paul Southard, in Los Angeles – while prosecutor Frank L. Stephen started building a case against her back in Twin Falls.

While working odd jobs, saving her money, and reportedly describing herself as a nurse, Trueblood managed to convince Paul to propose. The two were married in November of 1920. Although Paul, who served as a seaman in the navy, claimed he needed no additional insurance coverage beyond typical provisions, Ormsby learned that a policy had in fact been taken out on Chief Petty Officer Paul Southard – with Trueblood named as the beneficiary.

Shortly after they were wed, Paul was transferred from Los Angeles to Pearl Harbour, and his new bride joined him in Hawaii. Ormsby was in hot pursuit, having tracked Trueblood with the help of California law enforcement. Officers in Honolulu received a warrant for Trueblood's arrest in May 1921. She was picked up on May 12 to return to Boise, Idaho, for her trial – with her husband Paul at her side.

"She's been a mighty good wife to me," said Paul, who refused to believe the charges, "and I don't care if she married ten men before, and they all died. That wouldn't make her a murderess."

Although tabloids had already started running headlines about the gruesome tale, labelling Trueblood catchy names like "Lethal Lyda" or "The Arsenic Widow," Trueblood maintained her innocence as she and Paul prepared to catch the *Matsonia* out of Honolulu. Some reports claimed she was acting "like any lucky vacationer about to embark on an ocean cruise," her neck heavy with flowered leis.

"I am entirely innocent, and I look forward to the trip with optimism," Trueblood said in a brief statement to the press. "I am anxious to get back to Twin Falls and face my accusers."

At the jail, Trueblood finally granted an interview to reporter Hazel Pedlar Faulkner, with the San Francisco Examiner. Pedlar

Faulkner described the accused as "dainty, friendly, and refined" – not exactly the picture of a "sinister murderer," she said.

"I have been nervous because of my imprisonment and the unnecessary disgrace to my husband," Pedlar Faulkner quotes Trueblood as saying. "I know as well as anything that I can clear myself. The evidence gathered against me is purely circumstantial. Their work is to prove the charges, and that will not be easy because of the documents I hold."

Trueblood claimed that her husbands had died because she was a "typhoid carrier," and even stated that she had nothing to do with the large life insurance policies her late husbands had all secured before their untimely deaths.

"Life insurance was no object to me," stated Trueblood in Pedlar Faulkner's interview. "I have had enough money. And what insurance my husbands carried were business propositions they took out without regard to me or without consulting me, generally."

Before leaving San Francisco to bring Trueblood back to Boise, Ormsby and his wife, Nellie, took the accused for one last night on the town. After having dinner at a restaurant and strolling through a downtown shopping district, the Ormsbys and their charge attended a vaudeville show at the Orpheum Theatre.

Although Trueblood was trying to remain under the radar, a San Francisco Chronicle reporter recognized her – and wrote about her activities the next morning.

"With the grim specters of four dead husbands, a brother-in-law, and her infant baby hovering near her, while the accusing finger of the law points at her and charges murder, Mrs. Lyda Eva Southard, psychological enigma, calmly spent yesterday seeing the sights of San Francisco," read Herb Westen's article in the San Francisco Call and Post.

"She smiles, a trifle shyly perhaps, but a bored light creeps around her eyes as if to her it is all a tedious legal jumble, which will steal precious hours from her pursuit of happiness."

Up to the jury

Despite Trueblood's denial of the charges, the state contended that she'd fed Edward Meyer, her fourth husband, hefty doses of arsenic extracted from flypaper. Trueblood denied it and the state presented further evidence – largely circumstantial, but it was still enough for a conviction.

The trial, which started on October 3 and lasted six weeks, received attention nation-wide. At the time, it would become the longest criminal trial in history. Witnesses were called from Missouri, Montana, Tennessee, and California – a total of 182 named to appear, but not all were called to the stand.

Prosecutor Stephen tried desperately to bring in Buddy Thornberg to testify against Trueblood – a reporter for the Daily News in Twin Falls who had come close to marrying Trueblood shortly before she snagged Edward Meyer. He'd met the widow at the café, and she had swept him off his feet. According to reports, Thornberg had told his friends he would be marrying the "rich widow from Montana," and – on her advice – he was considering taking out an additional private insurance policy on top of the $10,000 government policy he already had in place.

After his friends managed to convince him to not follow through with a marriage, however, Thornberg had ended his relationship with Trueblood and was presumed to have moved to Washington – never to be heard from again.

An article claimed that "every session of the trial found the court auditorium filled to capacity, principally by women and girls." Another report claimed the trail was, "draggy," and "rather technical – arsenic versus typhoid, laboratory tests versus the official death certificate. This certificate, giving typhoid as the cause of death, was more or less (Trueblood's) sole defense."

The whole case presented against Trueblood suggested that she didn't particularly love her husband, and could have – and likely did – poison him. Not only that, she took out insurance on his life, and fled immediately after his death.

According to Ormsby, a visit to the McHaffies' home in Montana had uncovered evidence to back up this theory. He'd discovered a "large quantity" of cut-up flypaper containing arsenic in the basement, with residue of arsenic in a pot Trueblood had likely used to boil the poison out – before serving it to her husband in tainted food.

"(Trueblood) went about her killing very deliberately," Fanning said. "She bought out everything the store had in flypaper. It was obvious that she wanted to have a permanent supply on hand."

An article published in the New York Times on October 9, 1921 stated that under the questioning of Prosecuting Attorney Frank Stephen, Dr E. F. Roberbaugh, state chemist, confirmed the presence of arsenic poison in the body of Edward Meyer when he examined the body in April of that year.

"The witness testified he found .05 milligrams of poison in five grams of a specimen of several internal organs and .10 milligrams in a ten-gram quantity of the specimen," the article read. "The witness said the distribution of poison throughout the system was not equal and he estimated that a little less than five grains of poison probably was contained in Meyer's body."

He added that the findings "virtually duplicated" those obtained immediately after Edward Meyer's death in September, 1920.

The state requested permission to introduce further evidence relating to the deaths of Trueblood's other husbands, and the judge ruled the testimony admissible. While physicians did, in some instances, contradict testimony of other expert witnesses on the question of cause of death, analysis made by three separate chemists agreed that poison was present in all bodies exhumed.

"She poisoned their food, and over time, the arsenic would build up," said Fanning. "Most of the death certificates all said some sort of stomach ailment."

After a deliberation of twenty-three hours, the jury came back with a verdict on November 4, 1921. Trueblood was found guilty of second-degree murder. Speculation was that the jury had "blanched" at the thought of hanging a woman, but there was no doubt that she had done it. Even her husband, Paul Southard, filed for divorce after watching the trial.

"Lyda Trueblood was a classic black widow," Delong said. "And she did it for money."

According to an article in the November 5, 1921 issue of the Sacramento Union, Trueblood showed "no sign of feeling," and didn't even raise her eyes from the floor as the verdict was read. This was typical of Trueblood's attitude throughout the trial, however.

"On the stand, the accused woman maintained an unperturbed attitude throughout a long grilling by the prosecution, which failed to adduce any important admissions from her," the article stated.

Only eight years after Trueblood's incarceration, Ormsby suffered a paralytic stroke and died in his wife's arms. His obituary ran on the front page of the December 30, 1929 edition of the Twin Falls Times – and flowers were delivered to his funeral, sent from a Lyda Southard.

A "break for freedom"

Still, the guilty verdict and the sentence of at least ten years in prison wasn't enough to keep Trueblood from seducing men.

"She proved that no prison walls can hold her, and made her escape from the Idaho State Penitentiary by fascinating, as did Milady, a prison guard, who is believed to have rigged up for her an ingenious ladder of plumbers' pipes and torn blankets and garden hose," read an article published in the October 25, 1931 issue of the Salt Lake

Tribune. "This guard, however, died before (Trueblood) made her break for freedom."

According to the article, Trueblood had already served ten years of her sentence and was eligible for parole when she made her great escape on May 4, 1931. The ladder, fashioned for her by prison guard Jack Watkins, had been buried for months beneath the prison walls. Watkins had also provided Trueblood with a saw, which she used to remove a bar from her cell window.

"The escape itself was dramatic," the article continued. "Women inmates, evidently under the spell of the woman, who could fascinate those of her own sex as well as men, staged a party and played the phonograph and sang while she was gaining her way to liberty."

Trueblood ran right into the arms of David Minton. Minton, an ex-convict himself, had fallen under Trueblood's spell while he was still behind bars. After he helped Trueblood escape from prison, she'd ended the relationship. Leaving him alive was a mistake, however – enraged, Minton went to the police and told them they could find Trueblood in Topeka, Kansas.

This, however, was not before a nation-wide manhunt was organized to attempt to locate Trueblood, who was described by Warden R. E. Thomas of the Idaho State Penitentiary as "one of the most dangerous criminals at large."

"Some man will probably pay with his life in agony and death before this ruthless woman can again be brought to justice," he said. "That she is the modern 'Mrs. Bluebeard' is certain."

In fact, before the police found her in Kansas, Trueblood had managed to swindle another man into marrying her. Harry Whitlock, who later described Trueblood as a "model wife," was shocked when the police showed up looking for her. The relationship had begun when Trueblood, calling herself "Fern," had started doing housekeeping work for Whitlock – and she had suggested he take out a $20,000 life insurance policy, but it hadn't been purchased before she asked him for some travel money and took off.

Fifteen months after her escape, Trueblood was returned to Boise – with her marriage to Whitlock annulled.

Back in prison, Trueblood continued to seduce her prey. This time, she set her sights on George Rudd, a prison warden. She managed to convince him to grant her special privileges – frequent day trip to a local resort, visitation to see her sick mother, and even transportation to Boise to see movies. However, when authorities discovered that he'd been treating Trueblood to these privileges, Rudd was forced to resign from his position.

Free at last

Finally, Trueblood was paroled from prison on October 3, 1941, and fully pardoned only one year later.

"I think they figured that she had lost most of her good looks and charm, and was no longer a menace to society," Matthews said.

After spending a few years living with her sister, Blanche Quigley, in Nyssa, Oregon, Trueblood returned to her family's farm at Twin Falls – but the local townspeople and even her relatives weren't pleased to see her.

A few months later, Trueblood left for Provo, Utah, where no one knew her, and pulled together the funds to purchase a small secondhand shop. There, she married her seventh husband, Hal Shaw. However, once Shaw's children discovered who she was and learned about her unsavory past, he vanished – leaving her to move to Salt Lake City, where she worked for several years as a housekeeper and waitress.

"You wonder, did (the husbands) ever suspect that it was not a natural illness that was making them suffer in agony," Fanning said. "We can only hope that they never understood what was really happening."

Trueblood died of a heart attack on February 5, 1958 in Salt Lake City. Her body remains at Sunset Memorial Park in Twin Falls, Idaho, where she was buried as Anna E. Shaw. Still, some report seeing a ghost bearing Trueblood's likeness haunting the halls of the Idaho prison to this day – the prison's most notorious inmate, maintaining a presence even after her death.

"When she finally died, it was from a heart attack," Fanning said. "It's amazing to think that (Trueblood) actually had a heart."

GENENE JONES : NURSE KILLER

TAMI BARRETT

28

Genene Anne Jones was born on July 13th, 1950 in Texas but was given up for adoption. Her adopted parents had three other children. Two were older and one was younger than Genene.

EARLY LIFE

Her adopted parents were Richard and Gladys Jones. Richard, better known as "Dick", a night club and was a gambler. He was a big spender and generous when he was flush. His club was called the Kit Kat Swim Club, the place had a dance floor with a patio and pool outside. His wife Gladys was the disc jockey at the club and the couple lived an extravagant lifestyle. They had a mansion that looked down on San Antonio, would travel often and they would both have pilot licenses .

At the age of ten, however, Genene's father was arrested for stealing the safe of a customer who had been at Jones' club at the time of the robbery. These charges were later dropped.

It could have been due to intimidation on Dick's part. The man was six feet tall, weighed a solid 240 pounds and was bold. He had an aggressive demeanor when needed and his adopted daughter developed the same traits.

His business soon failed, however. The shady Kit Kat Club soon turned into a family themed restaurant which put Dick further into debt. He then sold off the restaurant and earned a living putting up billboards around San Antonio. Genene would later describe helping her father put up the billboards as one of the happier times of her life.

Still, Genene felt as if she suffered from neglect in the adopted home. The parents had paired off the four kids on the basis of age. Genene had an older brother Wiley and an older sister named Lisa. She had a younger brother named Travis who had a learning disability that she doted on and cared for. Nonetheless, she felt jealous of all the attention that Lisa would receive. Genene referred to herself as the "black sheep" of the family and took out her frustrations on her classmates at school. She worked in the library at John Marshall and was described as "kind of bossy" by the high school librarian as she would berate other student volunteers who weren't doing their jobs up to her standards. Short and chubby, Genene felt unattractive and began to become known for lying and manipulating people.

"Lying was like talking for her," one of her classmates recalled as Genene would often tell people that she was related to Micky Dolenz, the band member of the Monkees, and that she would routinely have phone conversations with him all the time.

Tragedy would strike in her teens, however, when her younger brother Travis died in a freak accident.

He had put together a pipe bomb which exploded in his face, sending metal shards into his head. Genene took the loss hard, arriving at the funeral with a large flower wreath, crying hysterically, then feinting.

"You wonder when Genene's mind got twisted," forensic psychologist Dina Foster said. "It had to have been early on in her development when somehow, someway she got a surge of power when she was care taking for someone particularly a child. This was probably her brother, Travis. Being a caregiver for him made her feel important. She realized that she could be respected and have people look up to her until it became twisted."

A year later, her father died of cancer at the age of 56 which further devastated Genene. She had yet to graduate high school and wanted to get married. Her adopted mother refused as she Genene's choice of mate, a dropout named James "Jimmy" Harvey Delany Jr as nothing but trouble.

The two would marry, however, and live in a guesthouse near the mansion. Jimmy, however, was only interested in cars and drinking. The two would squabble often until Jimmy decided to join the Navy. With her husband away a basic training, Genene would not remain faithful, going after both single and married men. She had an affair with the newlywed husband of a former high school classmate. Then she began to tell people she had been sexually abused as a child. After four years of marriage, Genene divorced Jimmy as she stated that he had been physically abusive toward her.

Genene would threaten divorce but the two would reconcile.

"She experienced abandonment twice," Foster said. "The first go around was when her mother gave her up for adoption. The second go around was when her brothers and father died back to back. She had lost two loved ones to illnesses and one to a tragic accident. She felt helpless and out of control. But unlike most people, Genene went the criminal route in order to assuage the pain. She had to do things to get the power and control back."

CAREER LIFE & DIVORCE

Genene entered Mim's Beauty School and became a beautician, finding work at the Methodist Hospital beauty parlor. She had her first child, Richard, in 1972 while she and Jimmy were stationed in Georgia. They would move back to San Antonio but by that time the marriage was failing. She filed for divorce in Bexar County, eight months after Richard was born and stated that her husband was "a man of violent and ungovernable temper and passion" while also accusing him of "unconscionable brutality and physical cruelty." She won a court order that forbade her husband from going near both her or baby Richard. Two months later, however, the couple had gotten back together and the judge threw out the divorce suit.

"Clearly they had an on and off again relationship," Foster said. "Jimmy was hapless, wanting to do nothing more than race cars and party. So in some aspects Genene had found her soul mate, a man who needed taking care of."

But on June 3rd, 1974, Genene filed for divorce again and the couple would battle in the court system for three more years. She would file suit against Delany for failure to pay child support and in August of 1976 she won a contempt citation against him. In March of 1977, both consented to drop the legal battle and in July 17 of 1977 Genene's second child, Heather, was born. She later admitted that Heather had been conceived out of wedlock when she and Delany had another brief coming to terms.

Genene would then move back in with her adopted mother who helped with the babies as she began her training at San Antonio Independent School District's School of Vocational Nursing. Genene was a mediocre high school student but she excelled in the program, earning high grades. She aced the licensing exam and got a job at Methodist Hospital.

Genene only lasted eight months, however, getting fired when she made decisions about patient care in which she had no authority as well as being rude to patients. Genene would later claim that she was fired for standing up to a doctor who was being rude to a patient.

"She was a compulsive liar when she was a kid," Foster said. "And the lying continued into her adult life as it turned into full blown denial. She was never at fault for anything. It was always someone else, doctors, nurses, her mother, her husband. She never lived in the land of responsibility."

REIGN OF TERROR BEGINS

Genene then found work at Bexar County Hospital (now known as the University Hospital of San Antonio) where she was assigned to the Pediatric ICU.

It is here where the trouble officially began.

Her first patient had a fatal stomach disease called necrotizing enterocolitis and the boy died after surgery. Genene did not handle it well, crying hysterically. "She just went berserk," Cherylyn Pendergraft said, the RN that was orienting Genene during this time. Genene went so far as to move a stool toward the baby's cubicle and just sat there staring at the body.

Pendergraft felt the gesture odd considering that Genene had barely cared for the child.

Nonetheless, Genene saw herself as an equal to the RN's on duty and worked extra hard to acquire more knowledge than an ordinary LVN.

She worked the graveyard shift upon hire then transferred to the swing shift where she worked f3 p.m to 11 p.m while frequently volunteering for overtime and extra shifts.

Genene soon took on a reputation as the "nurse who cried wolf" to the many resident doctors who were training at the hospital. She would issue warnings about a child's worsening condition to the intern. If the intern did nothing she would then go to the resident doctor. If that physician did nothing then she would go higher up the chain of command and wouldn't stop until her recommendations were addressed.

Despite her eagerness to be perceived as on the same level as a registered nurse, Genene would skip continuation classes on the proper use of pharmaceuticals. In her first year, she was written up on eight separate occasions for giving the wrong dosage.

Genene wouldn't let any reprimands stop her, however, as she soon became the ward bully in the cramped quarters of the pediatric ICU. She would intimidate other nurses with her coarse demeanor, making more than a few transfer out of the unit to get away from her.

Her bullying tactics enabled her to make the unit her own, as she was the foul-mouthed Queen of the ward, bragging about her sexual escapades and making inappropriate remarks.

"Here we see the beginnings of tacit approval," Foster said. "No one at the hospital wants to put themselves on the line to stand up against her. It is an environment where everyone is trying to cover their own ass. No one wants to play snitch even when this woman is saying and doing all of these inappropriate things."

Even more disturbing is that Genene would also predict which baby would die.

During "report", a time in which the nurses would describe the conditions of their patients during the shift change handover to the next nurse, Genene would play the role of the Grim Reaper.

"This patient is really bad," she'd say forewarning the nurse, or even predicting death."This patient isn't going to make it."

By 1981, Genene would always demand to be assigned to the sickest patients. She seemed to enjoy the adrenaline rush of the code blues and would grieve when the child expired. Genene would hold the dead bodies and sing to it, making sure she would be the one to take the corpse to the morgue.

"She had a twisted hero complex," Foster said. "She thought of herself as equal to any RN. Most LVNs defer to the registered nurses out of education and experience. But it was quite the opposite with Genene. When the shit hit the fan she would be the first to come to the rescue. The problem was that she created these situations where she could be seen as the hero. Remember she didn't give them enough medication to kill them outright. She gave the babies just enough of a dose so that they would go into cardiac arrest. She wanted to be seen as the savior to the parents of the children she was killing. She wanted to be seen as the hero of the ward. This need was so deep-seated that she was willing to kill to get that need met. That need to be seen as a hero. That need to be seen as the most compassionate of all."

TOO MANY PATIENTS DYING

Co-workers became concerned that a surprising number of patients under the care of Jones were dying.

"The other nurses became concerned," said Vincent J.M. Dimaio, the chief medical examiner at the time. "That there were increased numbers of cardiopulmonary arrests on the ward. All her victims were children. The most innocent of the population. This would not have happened if the cases had been reported to the medical examiner's office."

Unlike most hospitals, Bexar County didn't lock their medications in a cabinet. When it become apparent that children were dying in the unit from non-fatal illnesses, the hospital dragged its feet in an investigation. There was a two-week period where seven children died in the unit. These deaths occurred only when Genene Jones was on duty and the patients were under her care.

"Astonishing," Foster said. "The tacit approval now extended to the cover up of children being murdered. The hospital administrators put their own public relations and jobs above the lives of children. It is a travesty of justice that no one at the hospital was ever punished for this."

Genene had an ally in the department in the form of Dr. James Robotham, however. Known as "JR", a reference to the ruthless businessman from the TV show Dallas, Robotham was an aggressive doctor throughout his tenure in the ICU. He had no problem dressing down nurses or student doctors who were not up to snuff or did not bend to his will. He had no hiring authority in the hospital but took on a vital role throughout the ICU by placing the patient's care onto his shoulders.

Genene saw a kindred spirit in Robotham and the doctor took a liking to her. There was one occasion in which he needed assistance and chose Genene over another nurse.

"She had been validated," Foster said. "She also wanted to be acknowledged for her nursing talents and finally there was someone who came along and anointed her as someone who was worthy."

"Robotham's Pet" as some of the nurses would later call her, would nonetheless display a macabre interest when a child came in with a fatal illness. Genene would make it clear that she wanted to be on hand when death inevitably came.

Genene would enjoy calling the parents to inform them of their child's death, sharing in their grief over the phone.

"She was Jekyll and Hyde," Foster said. "With the nurses and staff she would be coarse, demanding and condescending. But with the parents of the children she turned into the ultimate caregiver. Soft-spoken, compassionate, and joining them in their pain. She would have the parents believing that she was the most caring person on the face of the earth."

Never mind the fact that she would orchestrate the medical emergency of the child.

"That was her way of getting attention," Dimaio said. "She was a 'big person'. She was a 'big person' when she resuscitated children. When she brought them back from death's door. And the rest of her life, she wasn't anything."

THE KILLINGS MOUNT

A six month old baby named **Jose Antonio Flores** came into the unit with non-fatal symptoms: fever, vomiting and diarrhea. Unfortunately, he came under the care of Genene.

The baby soon suffered a seizure went into cardiac arrest and died.

Genene grabbed the dead baby and ran out of the department with the staff having to track down the crying LVN. The infant was later blood-tested and the results revealed that there had been an overdose of heparin, an anti-coagulant.

No one had ordered that the drug be administered and now the staff became suspicious.

When questioned about the baby's death, Genene resorted to manipulation and blackmail. She told the staff that she took records on every child that had died there and she knew which doctor had killed them.

Finally, one of the doctors informed the hospital administration what he suspected of Genene Jones. He had found a book in her possession about how to inject heparin through the skin without leaving a mark.

The hospital administrators, however, did not want the bad public relations fall out that would result from being a hospital that had a reputation for infant deaths.

"Say that they expected one (death) a week," Dimaio said. "All of a sudden they were getting three or four or five a week. I don't think there was any doubt that they had a good idea of what she (Genene) was doing."

"The amazing thing here is that even after the incident with the Flores' baby, Genene was allowed to continue working on the ward," Foster said.

Another child came into Genene's unit, this time to recover from open heart surgery. The child made progress but during Genene's shift he died.

"They notice that all of them (the deaths) were on the same shift," Dimaio said. "And all of them involved patients being taken care of by Genene Jones."

More doctors complained and a committee was set up to investigate. Head nurse Pat Belko and James Robotham were in charge on the hospital end but an outside team of investigators came in to look at the problem.

This third party team declined to put the blame on Genene as their findings were inconclusive.

COVERING THEIR ASS

Confident of they were in the clear, the hospital reports no abnormal deaths to the county medical examiner. Still, the hospital knew that Genene Jones was responsible for the deaths.

"She was left on the ward even though they knew what was going on," Dimaio said. "Someone said why don't we just fire her? Then they said well she'll just sue us and they'll be a big scandal. There were more interested in saving their reputation and not being sued then in the life and health of these children."

In order to avoid a public relations debacle, the administration decided to replace the LVNs in the unit with registered nurses. They said they were raising the "training bar" for ICU nurses and that LVNs would no longer be needed.

"So when they adopted that policy they let her go from that unit," Dimaio said. "Let go by the way, with an excellent letter of recommendation. Even though they knew what was going on."

Genene had been suspected in the deaths of over 47 other children, the NYT noted that the administration of Bexar County Medical Center and the University of Texas Medical school had shredded over 9,000 pounds of pharmaceutical records, records that were created during the time when Jones worked there.

By doing this, these administrators effectively destroyed any evidence that would be helpful in convicting Genene Jones of more crimes. The hospital stated that the shredding of documents was "routine" and a "coincidence", but the district attorney was able to intervene when, acting on a tip from an informant, he stopped the hospital from destroying an additional 50,000 pounds of pharmaceutical and medical records. The dean of medicine at Bexar was then cited for contempt of court when it was discovered that she withheld hospital reports from the grand jury.

"This is certainly an indictment of the hospital," Foster said. "If over 47 children were murdered, than there would have to be justice. The irony here is that the hospital administrators are not that far off from Genene Jones' mindset. They lie, deny and keep things in secret. All for the sake of control. All for the sake of being perceived that they are something they are not. Genene wanted to be seen as a hero but was really a killer. The hospital wants good pr at all costs, even childcare's lives. They are scum."

THE MURDERS CONTINUE

After her release from the county hospital and with a letter of recommendation in hand, Jones found work at a pediatric physician's clinic in Kerrville, Texas.

"She ended up here in Kerrville after she left San Antonio because of all these unexplained deaths," district attorney Ron Sutton said. "Genene Jones absolutely despises me because I brought down her little self-constructed impact."

The clinic was a start-up to be run by Dr. Kathleen Holland. She only had budget for an LVN and immediately thought of Genene Jones. She had remembered Genene and had been impressed by her take-charge personality and competence.

Holland contacted the human resource office at the hospital and inquired about the availability of Genene. Holland knew about the strange rumors about Genene but was willing to overlook them as she needed someone who could bring passion to their start up.

Holland didn't know how true those weird rumors were..

"She would create these medical emergencies," District Attorney Ron Sutton said. "That only she would know to handle. Then she would look like this supreme nurse when she would take care of the emergencies that she created."

Holland's revelation began with Petti McClellan brought in her young daughter Chelsea. McClellan said that Chelsea had a "bad cold" and went into the exam room with Dr. Holland. Genene then took the young baby out of Chelsea's arms, stating that she was going to "play" with the baby so that she and the doctor could talk.

"She had an irresistible compulsion," Foster said. "Doesn't matter where she is at, a hospital, a clinic, she has that compulsion. She'll see the opportunity to be a create the scenario for herself and she takes it."

"The protocol for the doctor's office would be the nurse, Genene Jones, would take the baby into a separate room just she and the baby, to perform whatever cursory examination; weight, blood pressure, whatever," Sutton said. "But during the time Genene would have these children by themselves all of a sudden they would become like a rag doll. And then she would scream out 'the baby's not breathing.'"

Moments later, Genene would cry out for help, saying that the baby couldn't breathe.

Doctor Holland immediately jumped into action, seeing that the baby had gone into a seizure. The child would be transported to a hospital and her life was spared.

The McClellan's expressed their gratitude toward Holland and Genene. They thought the world of the duo, believing that they saved the life of their child.

Little did they know that Genene had injected the child with succinylcholine.

Genene had used various methods to kill children under her care. She used injections of digoxin, heparin and later succinylcholine to cause a "code blue" in her patients. She would revive them afterward and receive praise. The succinylcholine she used is a paralytic that causes a temporary paralysis of skeleton muscles which can affect a patient's breathing. When she injected small children with this drug, the victim would suffer from cardiac arrest.

Petti would later return to the clinic months later with Chelsea. She had actually called the clinic to make an appointment for her son Cameron but Holland insisted that she bring Chelsea in so that she could "check on her."

"My daughter wasn't sick," Petti would later say.

Holland later disputes the claim that she asked Petti to bring Chelsea in instead of Cameron.

Unfortunately, Petti would bring Chelsea in and witness Genene administer two shots. The second shot would cause Chelsea to go into a seizure and later die.

"Once she began doing it," Foster said. "She couldn't stop. She became fueled by the adrenaline. The rush she got by sticking the syringe into the baby. The rush she got in waiting for the child to go into cardiac arrest. The the rush she got by watching the child die and comforting it in its death. She even got off on informing the parents of the baby's death. That is how twisted her mind was."

"Her original intent may not have been to kill," Foster said. "She was all about being seen as the hero, the Superwoman who came into save the day. Why she would target the same child coming in for another routine check-up really shows that she was getting careless about her victims. She had gotten away with it for so long that she didn't care. Plus, the compulsion would override whatever logic and forward thinking she had."

Chelsea's death was initially seen as sudden infant death syndrome.

"That's when we talked to the anesthesiologist," Sutton said. "He said that this child looks like it was coming out from the effects of succinylcholine, and we launched our investigation at that point."

"Soon as she got that first shot," Petti McClellan said, "Chelsey immediately starting reacting to it. And I asked her right off the bat, 'what did you do? What did you do? Something's wrong with her.'".

Genene visited Chelsey's grave and seemed genuinely remorseful.

"She was a psychopath with conflicted emotions," Foster said. "On one hand she had this need to kill and be in control of what others thought of her, specifically as a hero. And the other hand, she may have felt remorse when her 'heroic' efforts didn't produce the results she wanted."

Chelsey's mother, Petti, however, was shocked to see Genene at her daughter's grave.

Holland would later find puncture marks in a bottle of succinylcholine in a storage cabinet that only she and Genene had access to. "There were two holes in the lid of this bottle," Sutton said. "One where she had withdrawn and then she attempted to replace it with saline solution."

With the investigators closing in, Genene began to panic. She arrived at the clinic after lunch and complained to Holland that she was feeling ill...She had overdosed on her anti-depressants and began looking lethargic.

Holland immediately called the paramedics and Genene's stomach was pumped. Later upon her release, Texas Ranger Joe Davis interrogated her about the holes in the bottle of succinylcholine. Genene denied involvement, stating that she would be willing take a polygraph test.

The next day, Holland was shocked to see Genene report for work as if nothing had happened. She then informed Genene that her services would no longer be needed. Genene grew enraged and challenged Holland to take a polygraph. She then stormed out of the office.

Genene would later call back to the office and informed Holland's secretary that she had left a letter for the physician in her drawer.

The letter was a one page suicide note that she had written before she had taken the overdose of anti-depressants.

"There isn't anyway to explain to you why things are going to change. Sometimes, as wrong as it may seem, you have to except what life dishes out.

When your older, and I know your tired of hearing that, but you will be able to understand why, why I have to go away. It doesn't mean I don't love you. Please believe that. No amount of money or worldly goods could every buy my love. It is so deep & strong, it will last for all eternity.

Please explain if you can to Heather & Michael how much I love them. It's such a strong love, I can't put it on paper. I know I'm asking a lot, but I really feel your the only one who could do it.

I'm not guilty of murder, & I hope you believe that. But Daddy's way is right. It takes all the pressure off you and the seven people whose life I have altered.

No one can hurt me with my Daddy. He'll straighten this whole thing out & then we'll go home & everything will be alright. No more problems for you, no more nightmares for me.

Please make sure Michael and Heather are not separated. I know how my mother feels about Heather, but I also know how she feels about Michael. If Debbie or you can't take them together, please be sure whoever does are good people. People with lots of love.

Please don't be angry. I'm going with Daddy because I miss him and I want to be with him. He'll take care of both of us.

You'll be fine. Please believe that.

I love you,

Genene

Genene had attempted to frame Holland for the murders but all evidence pointed to her. All said and done, Genene had poisoned at least six children at the clinic. Three of the parents continued to utilize Holland as their pediatrician while three other families sued both Holland and Genene Jones as they believed that Holland knew or should have known about Genene's murderous ways.

The criminal investigation began and Chelsea's body was exhumed, revealing traces of the succinylcholine.

Her exact numbers of victims remain unknown as hospital officials first "misplaced" then destroyed records of her activities to prevent lawsuits after Genene's first conviction.

Genene would go on trial on January 15th, 1984 for the murder of Chelsea and injury to the other children. On February, 15, 1984, Genene was convicted of murder after a three hour deliberation. She was given the maximum sentence of ninety-nine years. In October, she went on trail for injuring Rolando Jones with an injection of heparin. She was sentenced a total of 159 years with the possibility of parole that came up after serving ten years.

In 1985, Gene was sentenced to 99 years in prison for killing fifteen month old Chelsea McClellan.

Later that year, she was sentenced to a term of sixty years in prison for the attempted murder of Rolando Jones with heparin.

"I've had several cases that stand out in my mind," Sutton said. "But this one is particularly heinous because of death to small children.

SERIAL KILLER TO BE RELEASED

Genene Jones is now set to go free because of a legal loophole in the form of She is now scheduled for mandatory release in February 2018 due to a Texas law that prevents prison overcrowding. Genene has been a prisoner who has exhibited "good behavior", becoming eligible for the release.

"Please, please, please, do not let this person walk," Petti McClellan said.

"Genene Jones is probably one of the worst types of serial killers because keep in mind who her victims were," said Andy Kahan, a victim advocate. "Defenseless, voiceless, babies. One of the nation's most diabolical serial killers in our country's history is set to be legally released,"

"I was so angry that it went on for so long," Cherlyn Pendergraft said. "That so many children had to die."

Jones now claims to be sickly and is housed in medical jail unit.

"Am I prepared that she walks?" McClellan asked. "No. Because she's gonna hurt another child. I don't want to hear that she's sick. Or that she's old, she's two years older than I am."

"There is absolutely no reason for Genene Jones to be walking the streets," Foster said. "She has a compulsion that has to be satiated. She needs to be locked up for the rest of her life."

The current District Attorney is looking to re-open old cases against Jones in order to keep her in prison.

She Killed Dad

Jessi Dillard

Born on May 28, 1972, Stacey Ann Lannert grew up in what appeared to be a picture-perfect family. She and her sister, Christy, were raised by two loving parents. Tom, their father, worked as a financial consultant, and their mother Deb took on the role of a stay-at-home mom. However, as the two girls got older, their 'ideal' family started to crumble right before their eyes.

"In 1990, life as I knew it ended, for better and for worse," Lannert wrote in her memoir, *Redemption: A Story of Sisterhood, Survival, and Finding Freedom Behind Bars*. "I had committed murder."

Daddy's little girl

In the early 70s, the Lannert family lived in Cedar Rapids, Iowa. Deb was a devoted mother, Lannert recalled in her memoir. As a stay-at-home mom, she kept up with the regular domestic chores, but also spent a lot of time teaching her young daughter. Lannert learned her ABCs by the age of two, and at three, could write her telephone number and her name. Before she turned four years old, she knew how to read.

"We had all of her attention in the early years," Lannert wrote. "I wish we could have frozen time and just stayed in that place forever."

However, Lannert recalls being particularly close to her father – even describing herself as "daddy's little girl." Her father was "like Superman" to her, because he was always prepared to handle any problem she encountered. She remembers him as handsome, with a prominent nose and a strong chin, and a warm, comforting laugh.

"He had beautiful blue eyes that could melt or destroy me – it was his choice," she said. "We stayed up late together even when I was really little. He held me all the time when he finished work or studying."

After dinner, they would share a snack of buttered popcorn from her dad's special yellow Tupperware bowl. He referred to his eldest daughter as "Tiger," and always encouraged her to stand up for herself whenever the kids at school teased her.

"I always felt like everything was right in the world when he was there," she said. "He lavished me with attention, and I could see no wrong in my father. He was just *it* for me."

The family's life was so idyllic, so secure and happy that Lannert said she didn't pay much notice to the "tiny cracks" that were beginning to form in the family's foundation. A car accident that should have killed Tom left him with nothing more than a few scratches, thanks to his blood alcohol level.

"His body was so loose from the alcohol that he slithered right out of the car," Lannert recalled. "He didn't even remember what had happened."

It's not a big deal, she remembers her father telling her. "Everything is going to be fine."

But things weren't fine. The more Tom would drink, the more Deb would nag – and Lannert said the bond she and her father shared became even stronger as his marriage began to fall apart. And when Deb gave away Lannert's beloved dog, Max, she said she started to think her mother was just mean.

"Twenty years later, I found out the truth," she said. "She gave Max away because my dad would come home drunk, trip over my excited dog, and then kick Max. Mom felt awful when she heard the dog yelping in the hallway, and she wanted the dog to be safe. Meanwhile, there I was, almost eight years old, secretly hating her for taking my dog away."

After her eighth birthday, Lannert started to see a different side of the father she'd always admired. He started off by introducing her to a new game called "touch tongues," which progressed rapidly to more forceful activities like genital touching and oral sex.

At first, Lannert said she didn't mind – it didn't hurt her, and it made her father happy. She admitted that she also liked having a secret that made her feel closer to her beloved Daddy. He was "all I needed," she said. But when she was nine years old, her father's molestation got even more aggressive – he started raping her.

"I felt like he was just tearing me apart," she recalls. "It felt like I was literally being ripped in half, and he was saying such hateful things to me. I didn't know what to do."

She also remembers wondering if all fathers did this to their daughters – but said once he actually started raping her, she could tell "that wasn't right," because it was more violent and painful than the "games" they'd been playing prior to that.

"Any man who can hold his daughter down and rape her is evil," she said. "And nobody stopped him. No one."

Lannert's father told her there was no use tattling to her mom – according to Tom, Deb already knew about what he was doing to their daughter. For Lannert, it felt like a betrayal, and she began to blame her mother for the abuse that her father was forcing on her.

The bitterness Lannert felt toward her mother only intensified when her parents divorced when she was 12 years old.

"I became resentful even more so of my mother for leaving my dad, and almost even took his side in the whole divorce," she said.

She made the decision to continue living with her father when her mother moved out – even though he was still abusing her regularly, anywhere from three to five times each week. To Lannert, the abuse wasn't coming from the same man who she'd been so close to, growing up.

"At some point, I separated my dad into two different people," she said. "My dad, and then Tom, the man who would abuse me."

A deadly misunderstanding

A babysitter finally caught on to Lannert's discomfort, and asked the young girl if her father had been hurting her. When Lannert replied that he was, the babysitter tried to tell Lannert's mother – but Deb didn't think much of it. In fact, years later, she admitted that at the time, she'd thought the babysitter simply meant Lannert had been spanked by her father.

"What I felt was that he loved them and he would not hurt them. I thought he loved his daughters," Deb told ABC News. "I feel like I failed to protect my children … and I will never ever forget that. I will never live this down no matter what."

In Lannert's memoir, she describes how her maternal grandfather had "fondled" her mother, Deb – and, according to Lannert's account, the sexual abuse going on at her mother's childhood home also "was never acknowledged."

"But because allegations weren't made – the words 'I am being molested' were never spoken – the situation could be quietly ignored," Lannert wrote.

This kind of misunderstanding is part of the reason why Lannert now advocates for victims of sexual abuse – and speaks out about the value of teaching kids what is acceptable and what isn't.

"That's why it's so important to find the real words," she explained. "If we don't name it, people can make it mean what they want it to mean. If you say, 'my father raped me,' they get it. But I didn't even have that word."

Eventually, Lannert couldn't stand it anymore, and made the decision to live with her mother. But her younger sister Christy continued to live with Tom, which made Lannert feel uneasy. Christy had only ever suffered physical abuse at the hands of their father, Lannert said.

"I felt like I was protecting her by taking the sexual abuse," she explained. "If he'd hit her, I'd just thank God that's all it was."

When Christy was in first grade, the beatings began. After her father was killed, she told ABC News that by the time she was 12 years old, Tom was pushing to drink alcohol with him. And, she said, the more he drank, the more violent and abusive his behaviour would become. Even decades later, she can't handle revisiting the house where she grew up with her older sister.

"I don't care to see the stairs that he used to kick me down," she said. "I don't, I don't want to see the windows that I would have to climb out at night, so I didn't have to wake up being choked."

One day, after Christy called her older sister begging for help, Lannert decided to go back to the house.

"I walked in and opened the door, and there he was," she said, remembering how Tom immediately threw her down and began raping her. "When he got done raping me, he kicked me – and I got smart probably for the first time ever. I was going to fight."

That day, she said, was the last straw. One month later, the two girls snuck into their father's house. Lannert had argued with Tom earlier that day, and the sisters were coming home late at night – hoping their father would already be passed out. They often sneaked in through the window in the basement, Lannert explained.

He was passed out on the couch, but Christy accidentally woke him. He started yelling at her, while Lannert retreated to the basement to grab Tom's gun. By the time she made it back up the stairs, she said, he'd passed out again. Almost without thinking, she shot him in the collarbone – and he sat up immediately.

"All of a sudden, he just started yelling," she said. "I remember thinking, 'he can't get up, because if he gets up, he'll kill us.' So I picked the gun back up and just closed my eyes and pulled the trigger."

Lannert also remembers thinking that Tom "didn't deserve to live," and Christy felt the same way. She told police at the time that she "may have" told her sister to "just do it."

The next day, the girls talked to an adult friend about what they'd done, and the friend helped her get rid of the gun. When she called the police, she told them she'd come home to find her father dead on the sofa – likely killed during a burglary.

Eventually, though, Lannert confessed. She told authorities that she'd killed her father because she "hated him" and that "he needed to die." Christy agreed.

"I had this mind-set, 'this is going to end,'" she explained. "I wanted him to stop. I wanted him to know we're leaving and I can stand up to (him). I didn't ever really make a conscious choice. I guess somewhere in my mind I did, but I wanted him to know that I could fight against him."

She claimed the killing was in self-defense, but prosecutors argued that she hadn't suffered any abuse. In fact, even when police asked Lannert if her father had been abusing her and she told them that he had, no rape-kit test was ever administered. They didn't even ask for more details.

Determining the motive

One officer, though, had her back. Lt. Tom Schulte listened to Lannert's story after she made her confession. She explained to him that the many years of abuse had worn her down, and driven her to commit the crime.

"The last thing I told that young lady when I left her – and it was late that night, I told her, 'I'll be there for you,'" he said.

However, Schulte's testimony didn't support the argument the prosecution was making against Lannert.

The motive for the murder, prosecutors alleged, was money. They accused Lannert of forging his checks and using his credit cards – and said that with Tom out of the picture, Lannert stood to inherit almost $100,000 from her father's estate.

"I had his permission to use the account," Lannert said. "I wasn't working at the time, and he didn't want me working. It was a way of him isolating me."

Many people also questioned Lannert's choice to continue living with her father when her parents' marriage ended, if he was truly an abusive man. But she said that at the time, it was the only option that "made sense" for her.

"We got sent back and forth between the two of them a lot, and there were times that he didn't hurt me," she explained. "My father loved me, not the abuser who would rape me. They weren't (the same person) in my mind."

To Lannert, judging the decision she made as a child who was suffering through tremendous abuse does nothing to help the situation – and can make life even more difficult for the victims of these kinds of crimes.

"A lot of times, we wind up seeing more victimization because of the choices we make," she said. "My life was hell, and I was struggling just to be able to survive every day – and then, after the fact, I have to face answers of why I didn't do this or that. It's harsh."

Lannert also asserts that she did try to leave, moving 7,000 miles away to live with her mother on the island of Guam. But when she received a desperate call from Christy, she couldn't ignore the fact that her sister might need her help.

"All I really cared about was making sure that Christy never had to go through that pain that I had to go through, ever," she said. "I never wanted that for her."

She'd even tried to convince her father to let Christy leave with her, but Tom refused. According to Lannert, all he wanted Christy for was to maintain what little control he still had over his eldest daughter.

Lannert's lawyer tried to argue the defense of insanity or mental defect, attempting to use the "battered spouse syndrome" to explain her behaviour – however, in a pre-trial ruling, the court ordered limited mention of the term.

Still, several expert witnesses were brought in to testify at the trial and conceded that Lannert exhibited signs of abuse. The jury also heard from both Lannert and the babysitter she'd tried to confide in about the ongoing abuse – and, in some states, if a jury believed the allegations of abuse, Lannert's plea of self-defense could have been accepted even though her father had been passed out drunk when she shot him.

But in Missouri, the plea wasn't considered to be valid, since Lannert wasn't in immediate danger when she made the decision to pull the trigger and end her father's life. The prosecution was able to convince the jury, which found Lannert guilty of murder in the first degree. After just a one-week trial, the verdict was read – and, in Missouri, a conviction of murder in the first degree carried a mandatory sentence of life in prison, without the possibility of parole.

"The verdict was absolutely appropriate," said McCulloch. "It's the verdict that should have been returned. She got the sentence that she deserved, and that's where she ought to be."

For her part in the murder, Christy pled guilty to the charge of conspiracy to commit murder and spent two and a half years behind bars.

Despite having spent many years investigating sex crimes, and being the first officer to question Lannert after her father's murder, Schulte was never called to testify. Lannert admitted that she felt abandoned and betrayed for many years, until she learned that he would have testified on her behalf, had he been given the opportunity.

Once Lannert was in prison, Schulte said he made the decision not to contact her and explain what had happened. Any contact between them, he believed, would risk calling into question his affidavit – which noted all his observations from the night he had interviewed her.

Several members of the jury also came forward after Lannert had been sentenced, outraged that they hadn't been presented with all of the facts regarding the sexual and physical abuse Lannert had suffered at the hands of her father. A statement was issued by the United States Court of Appeals for the Eight Circuit after Lannert filed a petition for appeal, claiming that the Missouri self-defense statute indicates no specific time frame in which an act of self-defense can occur, following an initial act of aggression or provocation.

"It is therefore deeply troubling that the jury was not completely informed of the scope of the abuse Lannert suffered, her fear, or her rage that her sister may also have been victimized by their father," the statement read. "This evidence of battered spouse syndrome might have placed Lannert's actions in proper context, and may have allowed a jury to conclude that Lannert was not the initial aggressor on the night of her father's death, potentially resulting in a very different outcome than what she faces today."

Still, the court refused to accept Lannert's argument that "a man who raped his daughter, when she was in the third grade, made him 'the initial aggressor,' and the author of his own doom." It also determined that battered spouse syndrome cannot be considered a defense in itself, but rather indicates support for a claim of self-defense.

Released by the grace of God

After exhausting her appeals, Lannert petitioned the court for clemency for years. The affidavit from Schulte was a key part of the request. Her lawyers finally launched a publicity campaign on her behalf, which allowed Lannert to share her story to influential figures like Montel Williams, Nancy Grace, and Oprah Winfrey.

"Having to go public was the worst moment for me," Lannert recalled. "It was so shameful. How was I going to be able to look anybody in the eye again? But then I did it, and I started receiving letters from so many people, saying 'you could have been me.'"

Lannert had spent 18 years in prison before Missouri Governor Matt Blunt looked at her file. In January of 2009, Blunt commuted Lannert's life sentence to twenty years after undertaking an "extensive review of the evidence" – finally, after almost two decades of incarceration, Lannert was free.

"(I was released) by the grace of God and the perseverance of two wonderful attorneys, a police detective who never gave up, and a governor who had a lot of courage," she said.

However, St. Louis County prosecutor Bob McCulloch, who persuaded the court that Lannert was a manipulative liar who killed her father solely for financial reasons, maintained that she deserved to spend the rest of her life behind bars.

"I have not changed my mind at all about Stacey Lannert. She murdered her father for his inheritance, and solely for his inheritance," he told ABC News in March of 2009. "She was never sexually abused by her father or anyone else, and she ought to be back in the penitentiary, and shame on Governor Blunt for letting her out."

According to McCulloch, Tom Lannert was a "bad father" and a "bad drunk" – not a rapist. He claimed Lannert was "lying through her teeth," and that there was no evidence to support her allegations that she had been sexually abused.

"The only credible evidence of any sort of motive is that she did it for the money," he said. "And she's not going to get her hands on it unless she – unless she takes out her father."

To this day, Lannert denies McCulloch's allegations that she "spent wildly" and was only interested in the $500,000 estate that she stood to inherit in the case of her father's death.

"I wanted him to leave me alone; I wanted him to leave her alone," she said. "I didn't really necessarily want him to die, but I didn't want him to be able to... hurt us again, to be able to get us."

Throughout her time in prison, Lannert said it was her own dedication to her faith that kept her patient – even during harder times. Although she worked hard at maintaining a positive attitude, she admitted it was difficult.

"There were times I gave up," she recalled. "I really believed I would spend the rest of my life in prison."

While Lannert agrees that since she did "break one of society's rules," her time in prison was well-deserved – but she said she felt she had no other way of escaping her father's incessant abuse.

"There was nowhere to run to – I didn't feel like there was anywhere I could go that he couldn't find me," she said. "He would tell us how he would find us: the car was registered in his name, he could track me through the social security card number, and he would tell me how he would find me and I believed him."

Since her release from prison, Lannert has founded Healing Sisters, a non-profit organization and resource website dedicated to help women who have suffered abuse. She hopes her work will someday help to end sexual abuse in America.

"Secrets lose their power when they're shared," she explained. "I think that every woman who's been abused thinks at one point in time, 'I'm going to kill you.' There's power in the thought – but not in the actual act itself, and I don't think people understand that. Now, not only do I have the shame and guilt of what he did to me, I also have the shame and guilt of my actions."

She also now recognizes that a more powerful action would have been to turn her father in – to put him "in the defendant's seat," she said, "and make my accusations against him."

"I was free in my heart."

Still, during her time in prison, Lannert was able to do some healing – and was finally able to deal with what her father put her through for all those years. While she said she's certainly pleased to be out, prison made her confront many of the uncomfortable feelings she had been pushing down.

"I couldn't run away from my past at all," she said. "The compassion and encouragement and support that I have been met with from other women who went through the same thing just really made me feel like I wasn't alone."

She also kept herself busy in prison by investing her time in a positive hobby – learning to train dogs to help people with disabilities. When she was finally released, she met up with Schulte in St. Louis – and he asked her to train his dog.

"I feel a connection with him that I'll probably never feel with another human being, because he was the first person who helped me, who believed me," she said. "It took a long time for it to come to fruition, but he did stand behind me and helped. And I'm just very thankful."

With some closure on the situation, Lannert said she can now see that Tom, her abuser, and the father she loved were the same person all along.

"I had to, in order to forgive myself for the action that I took, because there were moments that I missed my father," she admitted. "I had to forgive him in order to be able to forgive myself – but there's a difference between forgiving and forgetting."

Forgiving, she said, gave her the ability to move past what she has endured, and finally look toward the future.

"If I don't forgive him, then I'm in prison – it might not be a physical prison, but it's psychological prison," she said. "You know, I was incarcerated, and I was free in my heart. The rest was geography."

Although she felt free in her heart, it's nothing compared to the true freedom of being released from prison. Adjusting to life outside of jail has been challenging, as Lannert said she's not used to being able to do whatever she wants, whenever she wants.

"I ask for permission all the time," she said. "I need to learn how to break that. It doesn't seem real to me yet. But I'm working on it, and I'm so happy. I can't believe I got this second chance at life, so I'm just excited."

While Lannert knows some people still won't believe her story, or might judge her for how she dealt with her father's abuse, she said she chooses not to hold it against them.

"Every person in America is entitled to their own opinion," she stated. "I can't judge them."

HUSBAND KILLER : THE TRUE STORY OF TRACEY GRISSOM

59

SARAH CAMDEN

Claiming to be a victim of rape and other abuses, a distraught Tracey Grissom would travel to her ex-husband Hunter's workplace and shoot him six times in the back, receiving a twenty-five-year life sentence for his murder.

Her defense attorney would argue that Tracey was motivated by post-traumatic stress disorder caused by her Hunter's constant abuse and sexual assaults. One jury member had even asked the judge to be lenient in her sentencing as they were not allowed to hear details of her Hunter's alleged abuses (beatings, rape, sodomy).

But what really happened in the years that led up to May 15th, 2012? Was she in fact the victim of years of abuse by a psychotic husband? Or did she want to cash in on his $100,000 life insurance policy?

INSTANT ATTRACTION

The couple would meet during a dinner party in 2003 in Tuscaloosa, Alabama. Tracey was twenty-one years old and going through a divorce. She had a son, James Michael, from the previous marriage.

Family and friends would describe the union as "love at first sight." Hunter was blown away by the young Tracey's blue eyes and facial beauty.

"For him, it was love at first sight," crime author William Phelps said. "She was gorgeous."

A whirlwind courtship would ensue and the couple would elope in 2004.

"In the beginning, it was good," Tracey told CBS' 48 hours. "We had a friendship. Just your normal, honeymoon phase marriage."

"He was fun," Tracey said. "And he was attractive."

Hunter was two years younger than Tracey, however, and his mother felt that he had jumped the gun too early in the relationship.

Her words proved to be prophetic as after only eight months into the marriage, the marriage went south.

According to Tracey, their marital problems began with Hunter's drug addiction.

"I had caught him smoking marijuana," Tracey said. "Doing illegal things could cause a problem and I couldn't risk losing my son over."

Tracey claimed that she threatened her new spouse with a divorce but Hunter gave her his word that he would stop with his drug use. She stated that the relationship improved and the decided to start a construction company together.

"I took out an equity line to start a company," Tracey said. "Which was Grissom Construction. It was all in my name."

Hunter specialized in building elaborate boat docks. He had an artistic eye and could do docks, stairs, and other accouterments. The business began to grow in short order.

"They're going to take on the world," Phelps said. "They're going to be entrepreneurs and they're gonna make it."

They then had a daughter of their own, Anna Grace. The child was a long time coming for the couple. They had been trying for a long time as Tracey had five miscarriages before Anna Grace was born.

"She was premature," Tracey recalled. "Her heart and lungs were not developed. A very stressful time."

Behind closed doors things were rocky. On the surface, however, things looked good. They had a young family and were making money.

"All-American family," Phelps said. "White-picket fence. The whole nine yards. Middle-class. Suburbia. Maybe the Prince Charming that she's been waiting for."

But again, this was only on the surface. Tracey harbored secrets of her own. One of which was her own addiction to prescription drugs.

"Psychologically, there's something being going on here," Phelps said. "There's something going on behind those beautiful eyes and it ain't good."

Tracey would often turn on on the children, showing off her temper. Then she would turn on Hunter.

"This would cause friction in the marriage," Phelps said. "And where there's friction, there's fire."

SETTING THE STAGE

Tracey would later state that Hunter would "act strangely" shortly before she filed divorce. She was a registered nurse and gave him an over-the-counter drug test. According to her, Hunter tested posted for marijuana, Oxycontin, opiates, and methamphetamine.

Hunter would later be arrested for marijuana possession but his family would insist that he never did the harder drugs.

Tracey would file for divorce in the summer of 2010 after six years of marriage. According to her, this would prompt physical abuse from Hunter.

Hunter had to move out but their divorce agreement would allow him access to the home.

"In September of 2010," Tracey recalled. "That was the first time he physically hit me. It (the abuse) got progressively worse. He had made the comments that if I told anybody he would kill me. I believed him."

Hunter' co-workers and family members would have a different take on the situation, however. His co-workers remembered a time when she tracked him down at one of the jobs and made a scene.

"She's screaming, jumping on him," Hunter's co-worker said. "Said something about him having another girlfriend and used the expression about, 'You are mine. I'll kill you. I'll kill you. You are mine."

"She's borderline demonic," Hunter's mother said. " mean, I absolutely believe—that she is that troubled."

Hunter's family continued to believe that he did not abuse Tracey.

"He did not have an abusive, an angry bone in his body," Hunter's aunt Gina said. "In fact, we kind of laughed at him because he was too laid-back."

The divorce was finalized in October of 2010.

EVIDENCE OF ABUSE?

Loran Richards was the first of Tracey's friends to notice the minor injuries on her body. She would inquire about the bruises but the answers she received were always evasive. Seeing Tracey with a black eye, however, forced her to try and get more answers.

"I said, Tracey, you may have terrible luck," Richards recalled. "But nobody is so unlucky that they trip, fall down the stairs, and hit their face on a baseball in the eye socket. So don't give me a lame excuse. You don't have to give me any excuse, but let's take a picture."

Tracey broke down. She gave her friend all of the grisly details, detailing the abuse she suffered at the hands of Hunter. Loran then became her advocate, taking pictures of Tracey's injuries. She would later state that she saw blood stains and other signs of abuse at Tracey's home.

THAT FATEFUL NIGHT

Now divorced, Hunter would arrive at Tracey's home on November 22nd, 2010.

According to Tracey, he then became enraged when Tracey told him that she had spent the night with a new lover.

"He told me that he was gonna kill me," Tracey recalled. Tracey stated that she tried to escape, running into the closet in order to "get away from the kids and to pray." Tracey's eleven-year-old son from a previous relationship was in the home as was the four-year-old daughter they have together.

Hunter caught up with her and knocked her to the ground. He tied a belt around her ankles and then began choking her.

Half-conscious, Tracey alleged to have been raped and sodomized.

The brutal attack would leave Tracey unconscious. She would wake up the next morning on the bathroom floor.

"I called Hunter," Tracey recalled. "I told him that I was bleeding and that I was hurt and that I needed help. And he told me, 'Fuck you. I hope you die.'"

Tracey wound up in the emergency room after the attack. Hospital records would show that she had a laceration on her head, bruises, and ligature marks on her feet.

Tracey would then be referred to the Turning Point domestic violence center.

Marian Waters would describe Tracey's injuries as among the worst she had ever seen in a twenty-year career.

Waters would testify that Tracey had suffered a horrific assault. She described her mental state as typical of someone who had just been raped; fearful, jumpy, fearing for her life.

Tracey had suffered a hematoma on her side that was the side of a grapefruit. She also claimed to have experienced rectal nerve damage which would require surgery as well as torn vaginal muscles requiring her to have a hysterectomy.

Police were called and Hunter would be arrested for rape, sodomy, kidnapping and domestic violence.

"And at that point, I feared for my life," Tracey recalled. "And I feared for my children's life."

A HIDDEN AGENDA

Hunter would be freed on bail but Tracey got a restraining order against him. She bought a gun and did not go anywhere unarmed.

She took photos of her injuries on the night of the alleged attack and texted them to Loran. Later, they would take more pictures.

Angered, Hunter would stop paying her spousal and child support. Tracey, however, may have had another scenario in mind for obtaining money.

She had forced Hunter to take out a $103,000 life insurance policy around the time their daughter was born.

On May 24, 2012, the day before Tracey shot Hunter, she would place a call to MetLife that was recorded.

"Thank you for calling MetLife, this is Pam. May I please have your name?"

"Tracey Grissom."

Tracey would then explain that she was angry that her husband stopped making payments on his policy. During their divorce proceedings, he had agreed to continue paying the premiums. Tracey stated she was calling to make sure that they had the correct address on file.

"Is there anything else I can do for you today?

"That's gonna be it!" Tracey said, hanging up.

"Well, May 14th was just like any other day," Tracey said, explaining the call to the insurance company. "However, I had moved four different times. Me and my children were running. We were running from Hunter. So I had called the company to let them know that they had my old address and to make an address change."

FALSE RAPE?

Shelly Standridge was hired by Hunter to defend him in the rape case. She would state that Hunter denied raping or even assaulting Tracey that night. Hunter did, however, admit to the fact that he and his wife had consensual sex that night...Rough consensual sex.

"So that night," Standridge said. "Hunter said that she was depressed and claiming she was going to kill herself. She was saying she wanted their relationship to work."

So she undressed in front of him. Her beauty was always impossible for Hunter to resist.

The two had sex despite Hunter having a new girlfriend at home.

Hunter's aunt, Gina, believed that Tracey wanted to kill Hunter before the rape case went to court.

"He had a new girlfriend, he was living with her," Phelps said. "He was moving on with his life. Hunter would claim that Tracey was jealous, obsessive, even stalked them."

"Hunter had moved on," Hunter's aunt said. "There was some court dates coming up that would prove that Hunter was innocent. There were court dates coming up that he would get visitation to his daughter. She had a lot to lose."

Tracey was on the anti-anxiety drug Klonopin. Hunter would tell his attorney that Tracey would take more than her prescribed dose. Because of this, she fell and cut her head. Hunter would then leave the house around 10:30 pm and go to his father's house. Tracey would call him hours later, at 3:20 am.

Hunter would state that Tracey had called to threaten him. She told him if he didn't want the responsibility of the children then she would make it where he would never be able to see them again.

Hunter's attorney did not know what Tracey's motive was for crying rape. She was very upset that he had a girlfriend.

MORE LIES...

Hunter would be arrested nearly twelve hours later, to his total shock.

Tracey would give her side of the story to the police which later is proven to be false.

She would tell police that Hunter had thrown her against the bathtub around 10 pm and claim to be unconscious until 4 am the next morning.

"But her phone records show she was on the phone all night, so she was never unconscious," Standridge said. "She was also using her data at 10:42 that night. She was using it again at 10:50 that night. ... She sends a text to her boyfriend at 1:49 am. She sends a text to her friend at 2:07 am. She sends another text to her boyfriend at 2:07 am."

Tracey would blame the calls on Hunter.

"All I do know is I was not the only person using my phone that night," Tracey said, suggesting that Hunter used her phone.

Medical records would show that Tracey's head wound was "purely superficial".

Only one suture was needed.

Furthermore, there was nothing on the medical record to support the fact that Tracey experienced vaginal and rectal tears. She did have bruises on her ankle and legs but the photos taken by police at the emergency room would not resemble the same photos that Tracey and her friend Loran would take days later. In the photos taken at the emergency room, an area of Tracey's body has no bruises. Days later, there is discoloration.

Tracey's attorney would blame the discrepancy on "blood thinners" which would cause Tracey to bruise easily.

There was also a discrepancy in her phone records. She would take a photo of her inner thigh, a deep bruise. This area of her body was not photographed by police during her emergency room visit. But on December 9th, almost two weeks later, Tracey took a photo of her inner thigh with the deep bruise

"He (Hunter) told me that he would make it to where nobody would ever want me," Tracey said after a 2010 attack. "I didn't report it because I thought he would kill me."

THE FINAL STRAW

Tracey woke up pissed on May 15th, 2012.

Hunter had been ordered to pay $2,100 a month for the rest of his life. He was not complying with the court order claiming that he was "out of work."

Tracey stated that she was on her way to a job interview when she saw a Grissom Construction sign out of the corner of her eye.

She stated that her initial plan was to take a photograph of Hunter at the job site in order to show proof that he was working as part of her litigation.

"I was getting ready to take the picture and when I looked up he was standing almost directly towards the front of the boat trailer," Tracey said. "He was looking back directly at me. He had this face, that's like mean - just, I don't know how to describe it. I mean, I see it over and over like it's right there all the time. He flipped me the bird, which to me was kinda like, 'Yeah I'm workin. Screw you.' And at that point, I panicked. At that point, I didn't know what else to do except to defend myself."

Tracey started firing. The first shot hit Hunter in the arm. He started to run and she fired again repeatedly. One of the bullets punctured Hunter's heart and he died of massive internal bleeding.

William Dockery was working with Hunter and was an eyewitness to the shooting. Hunter had turned to Dockery before the shooting and told him to "call the law". Before Dockery could pick up his cell phone, Tracey had commenced shooting.

Tracey then pulled out her own cell phone and called the cops on herself. She tearfully described that she had just murdered her husband.

CONFESSION

Tracey told detectives exactly what was going through her mind when she came upon Hunter at the construction site.

"Tell me about what happened," the detective said. "What led up to...what's going on."

"In November of 2010, he beat me unconscious and raped me...and, and left me for dead....and, and I finally pressed charges against him and he told me that he would make my life a living hell...and that's what he's done."

"What, what happened this morning that led up to you going..."

"I was going to work and I saw him...and he's been claiming that he-he's not working. And, so I pulled in there to take a picture of him...cause it was the truck that's still in my name...and the boat that's still in my name...and the trailer that's still in my name...He just stared at me and flipped me off...and I just went in there and shot him...I just shot him, I shot him, and I shot him."

Tracey would be distraught and tearful during her interrogation room confession. A few weeks later, however, she would call the insurance company to let them know that Hunter had died.

"Well, I was actually calling because I didn't know what I needed to do ... Hunter passed away May 15th and I actually am going a court case right now because it was due to self-defense..."

Hunter's family went ballistic over this. Tracey would claim that she had no money but she continued to pay his life insurance premiums.

"Even through the times when she's screamin' that she's destitute and has no money ... she continued to pay life insurance premium," Hunter's mother said.

"I don't think my sister concocted a story," Tracey's sister said. "Just so she could get insurance money. ... But that's all they (the prosecution) had."

THE TRIAL

Tracey's allegations of rape and sodomy would not be allowed in court testimony. She was allowed, however, to detail the effects of Hunter's abuse on her were.

Taking the stand, Tracey would lift up her shirt in court and show herself wearing a colostomy bag. She stated that she had undergone several surgeries after her husband's daily rapes wherein she suffered permanent rectal and vaginal damage.

Hunter's family was then allowed to speak at the hearing.

"This tremendous loss has changed me," Hunter's mother, Melanie Garner said. "And I don't know how to change back."

Chloe, Hunter's sister, had a victim's services officer read her letter in court.

"Tracey is psychotic," Chloe wrote. "She is the most selfish person human being on this earth."

"Every mother should pray every night that your son doesn't fall in love with someone like Tracey," Hunter's aunt, Gina Grissom said. "There have been lots of allegations against Hunter. We've never believed anything that has come out of her (Tracey's) mouth."

His aunt then looked directly at Tracey.

"Hunter was proud of his name. Why would you still choose to use our name, and bring it down?" suggesting that if Tracey hated him so much why didn't she go revert to her maiden name after the divorce.

The jurors would find Tracey guilty of murder. She would be sentenced to twenty-five years in prison.

One of the jurors, Janice Kelly, would contact Grissom's attorney Warren Freeman the morning after the trial. She had remorse over her decision and said that she wouldn't have convicted her had they had the rapes and abuse allegations been introduced as evidence.

"I feel I made a mistake," Kelly said. "If I had to do it over again, we'd have had a hung jury. We didn't get her side. She did not get a fair trial."

"We voted to convict because there was no dispute that Tracey shot Hunter," the jury foreman wrote in a letter that was addressed in the courthouse. "Jurors didn't believe prosecutor claims that she did it in order to collect a life insurance policy. We felt the shooting was a crime of passion, not for financial gain and that she should be sentenced accordingly. I wish we had seen evidence of the rape allegation. We feel that she just 'lost it.'"

"It's not fair, it's not fair!" Tracey sobbed as she was led out of the courthouse and to jail.

"We think the sentencing was too harsh," Tracey's attorney Warren Freeman said. "Considering you have the foreperson of the jury actually saying, we don't feel like she should be punished according to being found guilty of murder. Let's just say that there will be a basis for a new trial, and part of it will be something that the jurors saw that they weren't supposed to see and I'm going to just leave it at that until I file my motion."

"My son died running for his life," Hunter's mother said. "I don't know what was running through his mind but I hear him say 'momma.'"

"People who think that I murdered him in cold blood," Tracey said. "Either don't know the whole story or don't know everything that's happened.

Tracey was asked on CBS' 48 hours if she regretted pulling the trigger on that fateful day.

"No," she said flatly. "Because if I hadn't I would be dead. I truly believe that."

"She has a way of making everything she does look right," Hunter's aunt, Gina scoffed.

DEATH ROW GRANNY

It never ends.
No way.
No way am I letting this man demean and degrade me another day.
He's just like my father.
A binge drinker. And the binges were happening more and more.
He's on the road to nowhere and taking me with him.
It never ends.
First my father. Now him.
Fuck it.
I threw the cigarette on the blanket. I knew it was flammable.
Then I watched the smoke rise and smiled.

In Lumberton, North Carolina, Thomas Burke fell victim to a house fire which was caused by a burning cigarette. Investigative authorities thought that he had fallen asleep while smoking, leaving thirty-eight-year-old Velma Burke as his widow.

They didn't know that the fire was set by Velma.

Velma knew how to play the part of the grieving widow. She cried and gave the authorities the requisite crocodile tears. No one would believe that the murder of Thomas Burke would set off a series of killings performed by the seemingly kind and harmless church-going woman with the soft voice.

EARLY LIFE

Velma Bullard grew up as the second of nine children in the rural part of Sampson County, North Carolina.

Times were tough for the Bullard family. They would live on a small farm with no electricity, running water or an outhouse.

"They had to go outdoors," forensic psychologist Paula Orange said. "The entire family had to endure the indignity of going into the woods or using pots to shit and piss."

The home was small and cramped for the nine children. Velma would be forced to sleep in the same bedroom with her parents until the age of five.

Her father was a loom repairman (fixing an apparatus that was used to weave clothing) and an abusive alcoholic. Velma had an older brother, Olive, who were subject to his nightly beatings. Lillie, her mother, was too meek to protect her children from her husband's violent outbursts.

"She had the type of father who would not need any provocation," Orange said. "He would take out the pettiest frustrations, like not being able to find something around the house, and take it out on the children. Velma would become resentful toward her mother who was too weak or indifferent to stop her father from beating on the kids. She accepted his discipline as 'the way it was.'"

Velma would find school as a welcome escape from her dreadful home life. She loved her teacher and was an excellent student during her early grade school years. When she would return home from school, she took solace in the fact that her father would always arrive home late as he worked long hours at the textile mill.

"Her father Murphy had that Protestant work ethic in him," Orange said. "He accepted the long hours and low pay, seeing a kind of nobility in that. Only problem was, he would binge drink. Not store bought alcohol but homemade moonshine. After a couple of shots, he would be 'lit' and inflict his wrath on everyone in the house."

By the age of eleven, Velma would be forced to take on various chores around the farm. She would clean up the house, washing and iron everyone's clothing (eleven people). Her father would chastise her for not mending or sewing his work clothes properly as well.

"Her father was a stern taskmaster," Orange said. "Hell, you can say 'slave driver.' He would have Velma come home early from school days when the laundry got too backed up. Velma hated this and felt embarrassed. Her family didn't have much and as she grew older her classmates began to see her for what she was, a poor girl that was an easy mark for teasing."

Velma would grow to be 5'3" but gain weight as she got older. She would be mocked about her obesity, her shoddy clothes the gap between her two front teeth. She would also be called "knot head" after she ran head first into a boy at school which left a permanent contusion on her forehead.

By the age of twelve,Velma seemed to have taken on all of her mother's duties. She would cook all of the family meals in addition to performing cleaning around the farm house. She would miss school for days at a time as her father forced her to complete chores around the home before she could continue her education.

"Academic achievement was not at the forefront of her father's mind," Orange said. "Her mother was of little use because of her depression and mental illness. Velma was the oldest girl so she took on the duties of mom at an age where she should have been playing with dolls."

ANGER, ABUSE, AND CHURCH

Despite her father's verbal abuse and alcohol-fueled beatings, the family kept up a face of religious interest. Velma would be sent to Bible school every year until the age of thirteen. During her last year of Bible school, her father marked the occasion by buying Velma a silk pink dress with ribbons. Velma recalled the day as one of the happiest of her life.

The happiness would be short-lived.

Velma would claim that her father raped her when she was thirteen years old. She revealed this only to her pastor in her later years before she stood trial. Velma did not even tell her mother whom she did not think would believe the molestation took place.

"Things that went on inside our home when I grew up," Velma said. "Were kept inside."

At the age of fifteen, Velma continued to excel in school. Despite her chubby physique, she becomes adept at basketball and is pegged to be the team's star player for the upcoming season. But her father did not allow her to play.

"Who is going to iron these damn clothes?" he snarled.

The family then moved to Robeson county and switched from the Presbyterian denomination to Baptist. It was here that Velma would meet Thomas Burke and the two made it clear that they wanted to date. Once again, Velma's father would intervene, telling Velma that she had to wait until her sixteenth birthday until she could date.

The two waited patiently for her birthday to arrive and the following year Thomas would propose to her while they went to the movies.

Knowing that her father would not approve, Velma and Thomas eloped, moving to Dillon, South Carolina. Neither Thomas or Velma had any money as they both quit high school to get married. Thomas then went to work at a local textile mill.

"At this point, I believe that Velma began to realize that her life would not be that much better with Thomas," Orange said. "He literally has the same job as her father."

Economics forced Velma and Thomas to move in with his parents. This arrangement would last for a year until Thomas got a better paying job at a soft drink company.

At the age of nineteen, Velma would give birth to her first son, Ronnie. The couple would then move back to Parkton, North Carolina where they would remain in the same home for eleven years. Two years later, the young couple would welcome a daughter named Kim.

A CYCLE OF RELIGION AND ABUSE

The Burkes would be fixtures at the local Baptist church with Velma taking the reigns to teach a Sunday school class. But the prayers and sermons would do little to offset the growing ennui in the Burke home. Two years after giving birth to Kim, Velma would get hit by a drunk driver while crossing the street. She would be hospitalized for an extended period, suffering both physically and mentally.

Thomas' job at the soft drink company would not be enough to provide for the family. Velma would be forced to leave her small children at home and work in a textile mill just like her father. The couple would have different work hours, with Velma working nights and Thomas working days as they would take turns watching the children.

Velma would fall victim to the hard work at the mill and the stress of raising two young children. She began bleeding and her doctor performed a hysterectomy.

Velma's mother would take pity on the couple and give them one acre of land near their old farm. Thomas would build a three-bedroom home for the family but Velma was already going down a slippery slope. Her personality changed after the hysterectomy, claiming that she always felt "nervous and afraid."

Things would get worse as Thomas suffered a head injury in a car accident. He then began to drink heavily and begin to beat Velma.

"It was deja vu," Orange said. "Velma had, in essence, married her father."

One night, the couple argued and Thomas punched Velma in an alcohol-fueled tantrum. The police are called to the home and Velma sent Thomas to the state hospital to get treatment for his drinking. Her husband remains there for three days but when he returns home, his behavior is worse than behavior. He's angry at Velma for sending him to the "drunk tank". His alcoholism worsens and he would go on to lose his job because of absenteeism.

"Velma is thirty-five years old at this time," Orange said. "But she's an old thirty-five with crow's feet under her eyes and a hangdog look. She's had a rough life, not necessarily by her own design, and it has taken its toll."

Velma leaves the textile mill but then finds two different jobs in order to support the family. During the day, she works as a sales clerk in a Belk department store. At night, she goes to work as a machine operator in a cotton mill.

Thomas, meanwhile, would continue to drink.

He rages on a daily basis, on one occasion he pinned son Ronnie up against the wall and threatened him with a knife. Velma would faint during the encounter and be transported to the hospital. She was diagnosed as having a nervous breakdown and lapsed into a serious depression. The medical staff gave her tranquilizers to calm down. Velma believed that it was during this stint in the hospital that she became addicted to the painkillers.

"The drugs were helping," Orange said. "When nothing else did. So she wanted more and more."

Velma's children acknowledged that their mother's mood swings were due to the drugs.

Over the next three years, Velma would go in and out of the hospital for drug overdoses. After each visit, her addiction only grew as did her prescription list.

"She fell through the cracks in her own family," Orange said. "And in the system itself. Her family had their own issues to deal with as Thomas would abuse everyone on a daily basis. Finally, Velma did something she could control. She killed her husband."

On April 21st, 1969, Velma would drop a cigarette on the floor of her home and waited until her husband inhaled enough smoke to die.

His death, however, would do nothing to solve Velma's problems.

Her addictions and anxiety would only get worse.

A HOSPITAL FREQUENT FLYER

Velma would have another nervous breakdown after killing Thomas and lapse into a guilt-ridden depression. But seven months later, a co-worker at the Belk department store would introduce her to fifty-four-year-old Jennings Barfield. Jennings had emphysema and diabetes but Velma would marry him anyway. Unlike her marriage with Thomas which started out well, Velma's marriage with the older Jennings would be troubled from the start. Her drug addiction would escalate and Jennings would express his own regret at marrying her.

"I don't know why I married her," Jennings said. "All she does is pop pills all day."

After less than three years of marriage, Velma decided to part ways with Jennings. She didn't file for divorce, however, she decided to poison him with arsenic. She would later claim that she only meant to "make him sick."

Jennings Barfield was already ill and doctors had no suspicion that Velma was behind the death. Arsenic was a slow burn poison that could kill without detection. The autopsy called for no arsenic test and Velma had gotten away with murder once again.

But Seven months later, Velma would overdose on her prescription meds and become hospitalized. Her family recognized the pattern but could not wean Velma off of the drinks. She would remain hospitalized for three weeks.

Her personality seemed to change after the hospital release. She returned to work at Belk department store but kept being combative and argumentative with customers. Her boss knew of her circumstances and tried to coax her to do better. He took her away from the public contact and into the back stock room where he had her put pricing on the clothing items.

Her boss soon realized that Velma's addiction had gotten out of control. Velma would not be able to function in the back room, leaving tasks uncompleted as she would have her prescription medications delivered to the store.

"It is a hopeless situation," the store manager told Velma's son Ronnie before he fired his mother.

BROKE AND DESTITUTE

With no income, Velma would lose the family home as she no longer paid the mortgage. She would be forced to move back in with her parents and face the two people she blamed everything for.

Her father had grown ill, however, and would die from lung cancer shortly after Velma moved back into the home. She would feel bad about her father's death and admit that she had a love/hate relationship with him.

"I had learned to love him as much as I had hated him," Velma said. "He was so good to my kids. I think he tried to do with my kids like he wished he had done to us. He could not stand to see me correct them. If I would pick them up and spank them, he would ask me, 'Isn't that enough?'"

But after her father's death Velma self-medicated once again. She overdosed and was hospitalized for two weeks. Her family didn't judge, they instead thought she was "cursed."

"Velma needed psychiatric help," Orange said. "So she began medicating herself with deleterious results. She would "doctor shop" for different physicians who would be manipulated into giving her the drugs she wanted. Her addiction eventually grows until she becomes desperate for money in order to fuel the drug habit."

A MURDERER AND A THIEF

Velma began stealing from those closest to her, starting with her mother. Her mother confronted Velma about a missing check and Velma went ballistic.

"She had violent mood swings," Orange said. "The medication had completely changed her personality as she needed the drugs above all else. The people around her were not familiar with how to handle a person who had this kind of mental illness. So this made for a very dangerous cocktail for her and anyone close to her."

Hitting a new low, Velma took out a $1,000 loan under her mother Lillie's name. She put up the family home as collateral and forged her mother's signature on the documents. Velma then blew through the money and a month later took out another loan, once again using her mother's house as collateral. The following month, she emptied the checking account on her now deceased husband, Jennings. Two months later, the loan company began sending Velma overdue notices as she had not been paying off the loan.

"In Velma's mind," Orange said. "She had no other choice but to kill off her own mother."

Velma went to the local pharmacy and looked for bottles that had the warning of "fatal if ingested." She put the poison into a drink for her mother and watched as she drank the fatal elixir.

Her mother then began vomiting and lost control of her bowels. Within a few hours, her mother could not so much as walk and an ambulance was called.

Velma came to visit her in the hospital to finish the job. Armed with a Thermos, she made a special concoction of chicken soup and arsenic.

"Drink it slow," Velma said as she tenderly lifted the cups to the lips of her ailing mother. "Slow."

Her mother would eventually die of "natural causes" as no one suspected Velma of committing murder. Instead, she received sympathy.

"So sorry for your loss," hospital staff said.

"The thing with arsenic is that it shuts down the whole system," Orange said. "So hospital staff just chalked up her mother's weakness to old age. Checking for arsenic poisoning would be the furthest thing from their mind."

Velma showed the necessary emotion and received sympathy from friends and family. She then moved in with her daughter Kim and son-in-law Dennis who lived in a trailer park. She could not evade the authorities for long though as the authorities caught wind of Velma's check forgeries.

Velma reacted as she always did. She would run away and medicate herself.

"Her drug addiction kept pushing her into a corner and she saw no way out," Orange said. "So, this time, she goes to her son Ronnie's house and overdoses again, trying to kill herself. She falls and breaks her collar bone which laid her out in the hospital another three weeks."

But the police find her situation unsympathetic.

"We're sorry, Velma," the deputy informed her at her hospital bed. "But once you have been cleared for release, we will arrest you."

Velma would not have that. She tried to overdose again but this go around the hospital staff pumped out her stomach.

She was sent to court the next day and sentenced to six months in jail for the forgery. She is released after four months for good behavior.

NO REHAB HERE

Her addiction still unchecked, Velma returned to live with Kim and her son-in-law. She rummaged through the belongings of her son-in-law and stole a check, forging his name so she can get more prescription meds. Her daughter Kim now has caught wind of her mother's addiction, pleading with her doctors to stop prescribing her.

"In some ways," Orange said. "The doctors were just as guilty as she was. But back in the day, there was no way to cross-reference this stuff like we do now. Once she had her fill with one doctor she would go to the next and the next."

Velma's addiction prevented her from taking a forty-hour a week job. So she looked for alternative forms of income.

She would find a job taking care of the elderly.

Montgomery and Dolly Edwards would be her first clients.

"She found herself some easy targets," Orange said. "There didn't seem to be any legislative body in place that prevents sociopaths from caretaking the elderly. So Velma doesn't slip through any cracks, she just befriends the elderly couple and begins taking care of them."

Montgomery was blind and unable to walk. He was 93-years old and his 83-year old wife was too feeble to take care of him. They paid $75 a week for Velma to become their live-in caretaker.

All was good, at least in the beginning. But Dolly had a sharp tongue and would criticize Velma daily. Velma would keep a nice exterior unless confronted, saw Dolly has yet another wheel in her cycle of verbal abuse.

"It seemed to be a never-ending loop for her," Orange said. "Being forced to deal with verbally abusive people. Velma had long since snapped and Dollie simply had no idea who she was dealing with."

Velma began to plot out Montgomery and Dollie's demise until she meets their nephew, Stuart Taylor.

Stuart was already married but was blown away when he met the caretaker of his Aunt Dollie.

Velma would play it cool, stealing what she could from the couple in terms of petty cash and household items that had value. They outlived their usefulness to her within a year as Montgomery died of "natural causes". One month later, Dolly also passed away.

And again, no one suspected the sweet and soft-spoken Velma to have had anything to do with their deaths.

MOVING ON

Velma saw being a caretaker as a perfect front for her. She could steal as much money as she could and when the old folks detected something amiss she would simply poison them. After killing the Edwards' couple, she set the word out at church that she as available to be a caregiver. The pastor would refer her to Margie Lee Pittman who was seeking for a caregiver for her elderly parents, John Henry and Record Lee.

"She comes here twice a week," the pastor reassured Pittman. "She's a nice, kindly woman. You can't go wrong."

Pittman's father, John Henry Lee, was eighty years old when he discovered that his new caregiver had forged a $50 check on his account. He then fell violently ill, suffering through a spastic spell of vomiting, diarrhea, and convulsions. The doctors would chalk up his quick death to gastroenteritis but in fact, he had been poisoned with arsenic.

Velma played the caregiver role until his end. She attended his funeral and cried with the family, sending an ornate wreath (with money stolen from the dead man) to the proceedings.

For whatever reason, Velma spared Lee's wife and moved back to Lumberton, North Carolina to live in a trailer park. She began working as an aide in a nursing home and received word from Stuart that he was now a widow. The two began dating and she moved part of her belongings into his home.

"Stuart is a nice guy," Orange said. "He has no idea what kind of woman Velma is. She is so manipulative and cunning that the younger man is putty in her hands. So the relationship starts great as she reels him in with kindness and charm."

The couple are happy cohabitating until Stuart Stuart finds a letter addressed to Velma from the state penitentiary.

Curious, he began reading the correspondence and realized that is from a former cellmate of Velma.

Stuart became enraged. He threatened to "expose" Velma to all of his family and friends. Somehow, someway, however, she was able to calm him down.

He then found out that she had forged over $200 in checks on his account. The two argued but stayed together for the next two months.

"Velma had the Christian facade down pat," Orange said. "She asked Stuart to forgive her and the next thing you know they are going to a Rex Humbard revival. But before they went, she poured arsenic poison in both his beer and tea. She made sure he drank every drop."

Returning home from the revival, Stuart started to vomit on the drive home, the poison kicking in.

Velma had to keep the con going. She had to appear like a concerned girlfriend so she called up Stuart's daughter, Alice, later that night and told her that Stuart had came down with the flu.

Stuart's daughter expressed concern but Velma kept her at bay.

"Don't you worry now, honey. I'll take care of everything."

Stuart died the next day.

Velma would speak at Stuart's funeral and tearfully asked for his wedding band. His family graciously allowed her to have it and gave her $400 to help her cope with the grief.

But Alice knew her father was a picture of health. She vociferously argued for more tests beyond the standard autopsy and sure enough, arsenic had been found in Stuart's tissues.

On March 10th, 1978, the sheriffs arrived at Velma's home to bring her in for questioning. She was interrogated for over three hours, holding her ground. But she knows the evidence will trump her denials and tries to commit suicide after being released. This go around, however, her son Ronnie stopped her.

The sheriffs come to visit Velma again and she has one more surprise up her sleeve.

But Velma has one more surprise up her sleeve.

She would confess. Not only for the murder of Stuart but of six others.

"I set my first husband on fire," Velma confessed without an attorney present. "And I killed the rest of them."

"It was almost as if she wanted to be free of the guilt she had been carrying," Orange said. "Her confession seemed to take a burden off her back."

"The last ten years were like that," Velma said. "A drug nightmare. It was a case of not knowing where you are or what you've done."

The bodies of her victims were later exhumed and all tested positive for arsenic.

FACING THE GRIM REAPER

Velma's case would be prosecuted by Joe Freeman Britt, who was listed in the Guinness Book of World Records as the country's "deadliest prosecutor."

Velma would plead not guilty by reason of insanity but the court denied her plea.

"I needed to keep them sick until I could pay back the money I had stolen from them," Velma said. "I wanted to earn their thanks by nursing them back to health. I needed the money. I was addicted to pain killers. Anti-depressants. Amphetamines."

On November 23rd, 1978, Velma's trial would begin in Elizabethtown, North Carolina where she would be charged with the first-degree murder of her boyfriend, Stuart Taylor. The trial lasted seven days and the jury reached a verdict of guilty, placing her on death row at the age of 47. She was scheduled to be executed on February 3rd, 1979 but received a stay.

Velma would be sentenced to death and the verdict was appealed all the way to the U.S. Supreme court. Her attorney maintained that the jury had never been presented with the full extent of Velma's "addiction and background." Velma remained tight-lipped about that to everyone but her pastor. Her attorney felt thought her horrific background could have been used as part of her defense and the jury would have found her to be more of a sympathetic case.

CHANGING SPOTS?

"She's not the same person who went to prison in 1978," Kim Burke Norton, Velma's daughter said.

While in jail, Velma became a model prisoner.

"The first week I was here was the worst week," Velma recalled. "Everything about it."

Velma no longer had access to her drugs in prison and she began to dry out. With daily visits from two different pastors, Velma began to discuss her anger and repressed issues that fueled her addiction and murders.

Velma would claim that as she was awaiting trial in 1978 she came to a "meeting with Christ" that caused her to "change inwardly."

Velma heard a broadcast by radio evangelist JK Kinkle. "Jesus loves you, prisoners, too," Kinkle said. "He died for you too. No matter what you've done, the Lord will forgive you."

After Velma heard this sermon, she dropped to her knees and cried out to God.

She would then become the "go to" counselor for young inmates in the prison.

The inmates would nickname Velma as "Mama Margie" because of her wisdom and she would in turn think of them as her "adopted children."

The prison guards and counselors would take the most incorrigible prisoners and place them in a cell next to Velma. Velma would invariably counsel the young prisoner and advise them on the correct path.

"They'd come in ready to kill themselves," Sister Mary Teresa Floyd said. "And here she was with a death sentence, mothering and helping them."

"Living in prison is a struggle," Velma said. "Even at its best. And I know that without Him and His strength that has sustained me, I couldn't have made it even this far."

Her stay on death row soon became a part of the news brief. During this time, a phalanx of evangelists would take her cause to the mainstream. The Reverend Hugh Hoyle would become Velma's personal minister as she received stays of execution in September, October and December of 1981. She would also have a letter correspondence with Ruth Graham, Billy Graham's wife as well as meeting their daughter Ann.

While Velma impressed the Christian do-gooders, the family members of the victims were not taken in by her "conversion."

"She's got religion now, they say," Margie Lee Pittman said. "Well, she had religion before. So we all thought."

A few more stays were granted until 1984 when the U.S. Supreme Court justice Warren Burger granted her a stay until August of that year. At this point, however, her execution seemed inevitable. In an ironic move, Velma would choose poison rather than the gas chamber and enjoyed the final visits from her children and grandchildren.

During the final week before her execution, the Reverend Hoyle, and his wife came to the prison with a battery-powered portable keyboard. His wife played the little organ then the Reverend sang "He Hideth My Soul" and "He is So precious to Me" in the cramped visitor booth.

Velma sang along, whistling in the graveyard before the reaper came for her.

She then wrote letters to each of the victim's family asking them for forgiveness. Reverend Hoyle would deliver the letters to the families, all of whom would refuse them.

MEET THE HANGMAN

As her execution date neared, Velma was placed in a solitary cell that stood directly across from the death chamber.

"It's total isolation," Velma said. "From everyone I had been with for six years."

North Carolina Governor James B.Hunt would reject her final plea for clemency.

On the day of her execution, the jail house would turn into a media frenzy. Death penalty advocates gathered outside the prison and chanted "Hip, hip, hurrah...K-I-L-L" while some sloganeered with "burn, bitch, burn". The protesters held up a few placards that quote

Romans ch.13 which ironically was a verse that Velma would repeat to guards during her prison stay.

"For rulers are not a terror to good works, but to the evil...(The ruler) beareth no the sword in vain, for he is the minister of God, a revenger to execute wrath upon him that doeth evil."

The execution was scheduled to take place at 2:00 a.m but the protesters remained outside, their chants reduced to a simple "Kill her! Kill her!"

On November 2nd, 1984, Velma would be executed by lethal injection. The prison official came out and addressed the press, giving out copies of Barfield's statement of apology. The reporters then eagerly anticipated what Velma requested for her last meal. Initially, Velma just wanted the normally scheduled prison food; chicken livers, collard greens and a sheet cake with peanut butter icing. The last meal was delivered but Velma immediately lost her appetite. Instead, she opted for Cheese Doodles and a glass of Coca-Cola.

"Her attorney believed that Velma could have done some good in life," Orange said. "He stated that she could have become a teacher, counselor or a pastor. But her father set her on a path of self-destruction that she couldn't escape from. By the time she the left that road to ruin, she was too far gone in terms of her murderous acts. Justice had to be served in the end. In the end, the law doesn't care how genuine you are in your pleas for forgiveness. It only cares about the rule of law."

"I'm sorry for the hurt that I've caused," Velma said before her execution. "So many people, today if it were possible, I wish I could take every bit of hurt on myself."

JOANNA DENNEHY

When you take a closer look at the list of the bloodiest and most violent murders throughout the history, the chances are you will mostly encounter male names. Female serial killers are incredibly rare in our society. Women are unlikely to go out on a random killing spree and injure more than one person in a cruel way. When women do kill, they prefer using poison and their motives are very personal and driven by passion. Of course, there are always exceptions to the rule like Aileen Wuornos who became the most famous female serial killer. She shot and killed seven men in Florida over the course of several years.

You can only imagine the shock that spread through Peterborough, a small town in the eastern part of England when bodies started showing up in ditches over the course of several days. The investigators discovered that three grisly murders were committed by Joanna Dennehy. She was troubled but her life to that point only involved drugs and alcohol, at least to those who didn't know her well. Something happened and she simply snapped, going on a killing spree that frightened the entire Cambridgeshire, as well as the rest of the Great Britain. Her erratic behavior that escalated during those two weeks while she was on a prowl continues to puzzle experts and the law enforcement to this day.

Joanna's early life

Joanna Dennehy grew up in a middle-class family with a sister. Both parents were employed and they did their best to provide everything for the girls. Joanna's mother worked as a shopkeeper while her father was a security guard. She was very close to her sister Maria who is only two years younger than her. The age difference was insignificant and those two would spend all of their free time together, either singing or playing in the backyard.

However, everything changed once Joanna entered puberty. She began to rebel against her parents and her grades were on a steady decline. She would often come to classes visibly intoxicated. Joanna would run away from her home a couple of times, often with older boys. It seemed like her future will not be so bright. In 1997, when Joanna was only fifteen years old, she met her future husband in a park. His name is John Treanor and he was walking his German shepherd. He would later say: "She approached me. She had a thing for dogs – it just went from there. She'd fallen out with her parents and she was a bit of a free spirit but I liked her – in fact I loved her."

The two fell in love instantly, ignoring the age gap of six years. You can imagine that Joanna's parents weren't too thrilled about their relationship and they refused to allow Treanor to move in with the family. As a matter of fact, Joanna's parents kicked her out of their home in hopes she would leave Treanor and come back without him. But the pair was inseparable and they wanted to give their relationship a real chance. They found a house in Luton and lived with a couple of roommates in a very small place. Joanna continued to drink heavily while Treanor used marijuana. They would often steal food from shops in order to survive because they couldn't find a real job.

Joanna Dennehy was only seventeen when she gave birth to the pair's first child. Treanor was thrilled with this new addition to their small family and he got a steady job as a security guard, bringing the income to the household. However, Joanna wasn't too thrilled and she moved on to using cocaine after the baby was born. John said that Joanna became unstable in that period and would cheat on him with both men and women.

John left her and moved to Norfolk with their daughter but the pair would reunite once again soon after. Treanor just couldn't cut her off from her daughter's life. Joanna came to Norfolk and found a job as well. She was set on making a change and turning a new page in her life. That episode didn't last for a very long time and Joanna started drinking again. She even physically attacked John and almost hurt her then three years old daughter. John kicked her out of the house and Joanna started seeing a psychiatrist for a short time. She stayed away from her little family for a year and a half. Little is known about her life during that period but she was involved in prostitution and spent some time in prison as well. However, John took her back once again in 2003 despite her heavy alcohol use.

The pair welcomed their second daughter in 2006 and Joanna did her best to stay healthy this time around. But John noticed that she started abusing alcohol and drugs once again. She was very cold to her children and it seemed like she had no emotional connection to either of her daughters. She met a woman called Charmaine and two of them started an odd relationship that included sadomasochism. Joanna did have a history of self-injury but it intensified while she was with Charmaine. Her wounds were becoming more visible and Joanna did nothing to hide the scars from her family. She would cut herself all over her body, including the neck and arm area. A homemade face tattoo appeared on her face as well while she was dating Charmaine.

John moved out in 2009 after realizing that Joanna will not change anytime soon and that their children needed a safe environment to grow up in. She became more violent toward him and even threatened John with a knife. She would often attack her husband when she was drunk but the fact that she pulled a weapon on him clearly was too much. It was obvious that she didn't want to live a standard domestic life and that the girl John fell in love with was long gone. Joanna was mentally ill and her disorders were becoming more severe due to the alcohol and drug use. It was only a matter of time when she would go over the edge, either hurting herself or someone else. Joanna remained in the East of England, moving from town to town and trying to settle down somewhere.

Peterborough ditch murders

Joanna continued to lead a hectic life and she was given a twelve months sentence for an assault one year prior the murders. She stayed in a psychiatric hospital in Peterborough during that time as well. She was evaluated by a psychiatrist who discovered Joanna clearly suffers from depression. She was also diagnosed with an anti-social disorder and it was obvious she had a tendency to self-mutilate her body. When she was released from her hospital stay, Joanna had nowhere to go. She ended up moving in a small bedsit in Peterborough. The owner of the agency that rented her the bedsit, Kevin Lee, sympathized with Joanna and decided to help her out by letting her do some work for him. He had no idea that he would become one of her victims in a matter of months.

Joanna Dennehy's killing spree began on 19th of March 2013 when she stabbed Lukasz Slaboszewski straight through his heart. Slaboszewski arrived in the Great Britain back in the 2000s from Poland in hopes of finding better work opportunities. However, he began hanging out with the wrong crowd and abusing drugs. He was in the process of recovery at the time of his murder. Slaboszewski and Dennehy met for the first time only one day before the murder. He was certain that the two of them are an item and even mentioned to his friends that he had met an English girl. They made plans to get together the following day.

Dennehy invited Slaboszewski to her apartment and waited for his arrival. He was attacked within minutes and died right away after a single stabbing wound to his heart. It was Joanna's first murder and there was a lot of blood in her apartment. She was uncertain what to do about the body and knew that she needed help and made a decision to involve someone else in this crime by calling Gary Richards (also known as Gary Stretch) who was her boyfriend at the time. Stretch is a known petty thief who operated in the area of Peterborough for years but he was never involved in anything this serious. His towering stature made him stand out and Stretch was one of the tallest men in Britain at that time. He was obviously smitten with Joanna and covered her tracks by helping her dispose of the evidence.

Peterborough is surrounded by farms and fields so they selected a remote location east of the town. Stretch knew these villages and farms well so it was a clear choice for the dump site for Lukasz Slaboszewski's body. They left him in a drainage ditch and his corpse will not be discovered for weeks. After returning home, Dennehy felt ecstatic and thrilled after committing this crime. Her sadistic needs were met and she wanted the rush to last forever. Dennehy moves on to writing a list of her future victims and jolts down a total of nine names. She starts planning out her next murder right away.

Since no one has discovered Lukasz Slaboszewski's body for days now, Dennehy was certain that she had a complete control of the situation. She moves into another house owned by Kevin Lee who rented her a bedsit when she moved to Peterborough. The two have begun to see each other occasionally and Dennehy was regarded as Lee's lover. After the move, she meets John Chapman. He was a navy veteran who lived in the same housing complex and also was Dennehy's roommate. Two of them became somewhat friendly because Chapman was also addicted to alcohol. However, Dennehy turned on Chapman and threatened that she would say Kevin Lee about his excessive drinking. She wanted to get him kicked out of the housing and loved the control she had over him because of that. They had a third roommate Leslie Layton who would soon enough become Dennehy's second accomplice.

Joanna Dennehy moved quickly. The plan was to make John Chapman very drunk and Dennehy would enter his room and murder him. Ten days after the murder of Lukasz Slaboszewski, Layton and Stretch spent a day with Chapman and the two men left the shared housing after a couple of hours. They were drinking alcohol and talking. Once Chapman retreated to his room, Dennehy grabbed her switch knife and sneaked in. She jumped on unsuspecting Chapman and continues to stab him six times. It is clear that she is becoming more and more violent because this crime speaks of anger and fury she feels toward the man as well as the enjoyment of taking someone else's life. She was escalating in a way that is uncommon for a female killer. Dennehy would then call Gary Stretch and sing 'Oops I Did It Again' over the phone which is a proof of her bizarre behavior. The photos of Chapman's dead body will be found on Leslie Layton's phone and they would help the investigators determine the estimated time of death. Those photographs would also serve as evidence against Layton and his involvement in the murders.

Gary Stretch cleaned up the crime scene once again even though Dennehy didn't ask him directly to do so. It seems like Dennehy wasn't too concerned about people finding out while Stretch clearly understood the consequences of her actions. The investigators would later suspect that she choose Chapman as her next victim because he was 'an easy kill' for her due to his alcoholism and she felt the need to go through the process once again. It was also an urgency to continue her killing spree as soon as possible. The next name on her list was Kevin Lee, her landlord, and occasional lover. Dennehy didn't want to wait for days like before and needed to kill right away. So she made a call to Lee, inviting him over. He didn't suspect anything because they have met before in similar circumstances and Lee expected a sexual encounter between the two of them. He fell for Dennehy's charismatic personality and couldn't imagine that something sinister could happen to him. Unfortunately, he was very wrong.

Chapman's body was still in the house when Kevin Lee arrived. He knew that Joanna was unpredictable so when she asked him to put on a sequined black dress, he saw it as a harmless game. Once they start making out, Dennehy pulls out her knife and starts stabbing Lee. He had multiple wounds all over his body and this murder was done in a deranged frenzy. Dennehy calls Stretch and Layton once again and the trio drags Lee's body into his own car. Dennehy is oddly proud of murdering Lee and she wants his corpse to be feound quicker. They leave him in a ditch but also position his body in a very humiliating pose. The sequined dress stayed on him.

They drive away and purchase gasoline in order to set fire to Lee's car. The trio is doing everything in order to cover up their tracks and destroy the evidence. They still had the body of John Chapman to get rid of. After they burned Lee's car, they returned to the housing unit and loaded Chapman into a vehicle. Three of them go straight to the place where Stretch and Dennehy left Slaboszewski's body. They lay two men next to each other and didn't even bother to clean up anything. None of them cared a lot about getting caught at this point.

On 30th of March 2013, a local farmer was going around doing his daily chores when he discovered a horrific sight. It was the body of Kevin Lee laying in a ditch. The police were called immediately and the team arrives straight from Peterborough. They identify the body right away but they are unable to find substantial physical evidence about the perpetrators of this crime. Since this is the area outside of the residential parts of Peterborough, there are no cameras that could have captured the criminal who committed this murder. They are shocked at the ferocity and the number of stab wounds he has on his body. The law enforcement was certain that a male killer was behind this.

Joanna wanted to kill again but she knew that doing that in Peterborough would be very dangerous. She suspected that the police are already looking for Kevin Lee. After all, he was a family man and his wife and children are probably worried for him. Joanna makes a decision to drive to another town with Stretch. They were both fleeing Peterborough as well as planning to find new targets.

The law enforcement starts digging into Lee's life and relationships. White Lee's wife is oblivious to his affair with Dennehy, his friends do tell the police about her. They soon discover that Joanna Dennehy is friends with some shady characters, namely Gary Stretch. Since he already has a history of criminal behavior, they assumed he was their prime suspect while Joanna might be the link to Kevin Lee and also his unwilling accomplice. After all, Gary Stretch is extremely tall and bulky so he could have overpowered Lee easily. They cannot locate either of them so it is clear that the pair is on the run from the police.

The madness in Hereford

Dennehy and Stretch make a quick stop at a gas station and they rob it. They are caught on the surveillance cameras and the police who already linked Stretch and Dennehy to the murder of Kevin Lee are closing in on their location. The couple arrives at Hereford which is a town located west of Peterborough. Dennehy needed to find her next victim so they cruised the streets of Hereford in hopes of finding a target. Joanna's mental state was completely out of control and Stretch would later tell the police that she said: "I want my fun. I need you to get my fun."

They noticed a man walking a dog and they drove up to him. The man's name is Robin Bereza and he is sixty-four years old at that time. Dennehy jumps out of the vehicle with her knife and attacks the man. She repeats her modus operandi and stabs Bereza ferociously then leaves him to die on the street. There were plenty of witnesses around and the police were contacted immediately. The pair drives away and locks in on another victim very quickly. John Rogers was also walking a dog and Dennehy did the exact same thing – scaring the fifty-six years old man by jumping out of the car and launching herself on top of him. He was easily overpowered and Dennehy wounded him badly. Luckily, both Bereza and Rogers did survive these attacks because the police and the emergency acted swiftly.

Hereford police issued a warrant and they were on a lookout for the vehicle that was described by the eye-witnesses. Soon enough they get a tip about the car and a patrol is dispatched there. The police officers discover Dennehy sitting on a passenger seat. Stretch was nowhere to be found. She was completely covered in blood and held a knife in her hands. However, Joanna remained composed and calm. She didn't make any attempts to get away or run from the police. They transported her to the police station and started the interview about the involvement with the murder of Kevin Lee, as well as the random attacks on residents of Hereford. Police caught up with Gary Stretch outside of Hereford and he was escorted to the same station. The police started questioning him but they soon realized that Stretch was just an accomplice. He knew how interrogations worked and he didn't provide the police with any extra information. However, the detectives noticed that Gary Stretch simply wasn't too clever to go on a killing spree for weeks and avoid the authorities. They came to a conclusion that their prime suspect is sitting in the adjacent room and as odd as it seemed at that time, the murderer was a woman. It was evident that this was an unusual crime that will become even more grisly after the discovery of Chapman and Slaboszewski.

Less than twenty-four hours after the arrest, another farmer discovered two corpses in a ditch outside Peterborough. The law enforcement arrived at the scene and they noticed the similarities between these two bodies and the murder of Kevin Lee. The wounds were almost identical and the fact that they were left in a remote drainage ditch suggested that the three murders are linked. As soon as they identified the victims, they made a connection to Dennehy. It was obvious that they had one of the rarest killers on their hands and luckily, she was caught and couldn't do harm to anyone else.

The examination and the trial

Joanna Dennehy is a unique murderer because a female killer rarely shows open acts of violence toward her victims. During the police interrogation, Dennehy clearly stated that she didn't want to murder women. However, the list which was found in her room said otherwise. The fourth name is of a woman who lived with Gary Stretch at the time. The motives shocked the investigators because Dennehy said her only goal was entertainment. The psychiatric evaluation would discover that Dennehy suffers from borderline personality as well as psychopathic disorder and that she feels the need to always be in control. She enjoyed hurting other people and being the one in charge. She didn't feel any remorse for her actions.

When there is a team of killers consisting of a male and female, the man is usually the one who gives orders. So when the detectives discovered that there was a second accomplice involved in the crime, they were baffled. Joanna appeared in front of a judge in November of 2013. The public expected that she would plead not guilty. She once again shocked everyone by admitting her involvement in the murders. It was a way to keep everyone interested and on their toes. Joanna loved the attention and being in the public eye.

Both Gary Stretch and Leslie Layton were charged with helping Joanna during her killing spree. They weren't called as witnesses during Joanna's trial. Two of them appeared in court in February of 2014 and were found guilty. Gary Richards also known as Stretch got a harsher punishment and was sentenced to nineteen years behind the bars with the possibility of release. On the other hand, Leslie Layton got fourteen years for covering up the evidence and not informing the authorities of the crimes that were taking place in his place of residence.

Joanna's court date was on 24th of February 2014 and she was sentenced to life in prison without the possibility of the parole. After the psychological assessment, it was obvious that Dennehy cannot be rehabilitated. Her mental disorders are too severe and she lacks the empathy and emotions towards other people. Her younger sister Maria wasn't too surprised with the judge's decision. She would later say: "I think the people, the drugs and the environment she went into triggered something dark inside her." Joanna joined the ranks of the most notorious female killers in the Great Britain because there were only two similar punishments in the history of this country – Myra Hindley who assisted Ian Brady with the infamous moor murders and Rosemary West.

Escape plan

Before she was scheduled to appear in court for her final sentencing, Joanna Dennehy started planning her escape from prison. She wrote down every last detail in her diary which was found by the guards who were shocked by the contents. Since the prison featured biometric locks, Dennehy wanted to grab one of the guards and cut off their finger in order to get through the security checks using their fingerprints. It was unclear if she wanted to murder a guard or injure them. Due to this event, Joanna was placed in the solitary confinement even before the trial itself and remained there until the autumn of 2015.

She would later contact the High Court and say that her human rights were being violated by keeping her in the solitary confinement for a long stretch of time. Dennehy told the judges she was becoming even more depressed in isolation which led to severe self-harm episodes. The High Court dismissed these claims and went public by saying that everything was done according to the law and that the punishment was justified for plotting an escape.

Aftermath

The police investigators were under the media and public scrutiny after it was revealed that Joanna Dennehy was allegedly surveilled because she owned a dangerous dog at that time and kept it in the bedsit. It seemed like she was capable of passing by the unsuspecting police officers without any troubles. The people wondered if there was something that could have been done in order to prevent these murders.

Joanna is currently in Bronzefield Prison located in Surrey. She is not in solitary confinement but still locked away from other inmates. Dennehy is still fighting for her rights that were allegedly violated after the guards discovered her diary as well as the fact that she is still segregated from the rest of the prison population. Sources from Bronzefield Prison claim that she enjoys watching reality shows, especially those that include food preparation and that Joanna is working on her own cooking skills.

Regardless of her current interests and how normal Joanna might appear, it is safe to say that the combination of the mental disorders she suffers from is deadly to anyone who gets close to her. She will probably never be fit to rejoin the society so the fact that Joanna is behind the bars is a relief to many.

COLD BLOODED KILLER
CHRISTINA WALTERS

102

JENNIFER MARTIN

Christina "Shea" Walters: Cold Blooded Killer or Victim of Circumstance?

The Crime

It was a typical, hot August North Carolina night on August 17, 1998. Eighteen-year-old Tracy Lambert and her twenty-one-year-old friend, Susan Moore, were planning a night out on the town. The two vibrant, young blondes did their hair and make-up together and made plans to meet with friends. They got into Moore's car, and headed out toward their meeting place.

Suddenly, they were being tailed by an angry group of young strangers. The strangers were waving guns out the window, flashing their headlights, and yelling. Moore attempted to flee the group, but in a moment of terrified disorientation, she pulled down a dead-end road. Three young men approached the vehicle with guns drawn and forced the women into the trunk of Moore's car. The vehicle began moving with one of the young men behind the steering wheel. When it stopped, the men opened the trunk and demanded the women hand over their jewelry. Once all the jewelry was taken from the women, the trunk was again closed and the car began moving once again.

The second time the car stopped, the trunk was opened to reveal a larger group against the back drop of a trailer park. The group began discussing how to "dispose" of the women, causing Lambert to cry out and plead for mercy. A young American Indian woman expressed disgust with Lambert's "pathetic whimpering," and slammed the trunk door back shut. The men piled back into Moore's car while the rest of the group got into a second vehicle. The cars followed one another into an open, rural area where Lambert and Moore were forced out of the car. Each of the women was dragged into the open by one of the men who had committed the carjacking. Moore began pleading for their lives. She reportedly asked the men, "What are you going to do to us? Are you going to kill us?" She followed the question by trying to compromise, stating, "We don't know what you look like. Just let us go." At that point, one man held a gun to Tracy Lambert's head and said, "Well, I'm about to open this bitch's third eye." Lambert then started crying and said, "Oh, my god, Susan. We're going to die. We're going to die. I don't want to die." The gunman then told Tracy to "Shut up" before shooting her in the head. Another man was holding onto Moore with a knife to her throat as she watched her friend be killed. She began sobbing and begged him not to cut her throat, offering to him that he could just shoot her, instead. He showed mercy in that one small instance and borrowed the gun from his friend, ending her life instantly.

By midnight, friends and family were already concerned that the women had not arrived at the social gathering and began to look. An anonymous phone call alerted the police that the caller had "seen some people get shot." Sometime around dawn, the bodies were reported as discovered.

Earlier that same night, Debra Cheeseborough was leaving work at Bojangles when a young man, his face hidden beneath a bandana, approached her, placed a gun to her side, and told her if she'd cooperate, he would not hurt her. He ordered her into the trunk of her own car, where she lay still, quietly praying as a group of young people, all unidentifiable beneath their bandana masks, climbed into her car and began driving. Presumably as they dug through the contents of her purse and glove box, one of the young men came to the realization that he had gone to school with Debra's daughter.

Debra felt a glimmer of hope in that instant. She thought that, maybe, because they had made a connection, they would let her go without harming her. That hope was crushed when she heard the young people joking about how they had disliked her daughter and how much fun it was going to be to get rid of her mother.

The group pulled the car into an isolated area of Fort Bragg and ordered Debra from the trunk. She cried and pleaded for her life to no avail. Several of the young people, each with their own gun, began firing bullets into her. She was shot all over her body until the group was confident that she was dead. They left her lying on the ground and drove away in her car.

Debra later testified that, as she laid in the field, she could hear the voice of her deceased mother comforting her. "She told me it wasn't my time yet," she said under oath. "She told me she was going to help me get to the road, but not too close where someone could hit me." Debra did manage to drag herself to the roadside, where she was spotted by a passing motorist. She survived her injuries that night and went on to testify against her attackers in court, ultimately putting many of them away for life.

The night of August 17, 1998 was, no doubt, life altering for all parties involved in the events that unfolded in Fayetteville, North Carolina. This included twenty-year-old Christina "Shea" Walter. On the night of the crime spree, Christina had gathered at her trailer home at 1386

Davis Street in Fayetteville along with friends Francisco Tirado, Eric Queen, John Juarbe, Tameika Douglas, Ione Black, Carlos Nevills, Darryl Tucker, and Carlos Frink. Having grown up on the "wrong side of the tracks," all nine of the young people who gathered at the trailer had aligned themselves with the "Crip" gang, although they each claimed different "sets" or subgroups of the gang. The subgroups had come together and realized that the gang, as a whole, was in need of money. They formulated a plan to steal a car and drive it through the front window of a pawn shop, where they would steal the inventory.

Earlier in the afternoon, the nine friends had gone to Wal-Mart. They bought bullets with which they were going to carry out their plan and stole clothing and toiletries. When they arrived back at the trailer, Tirado borrowed Christina's blue fingernail polish to color the tips of the bullets blue. This was symbolic, the group agreed, of the "Crips" gang.

After discussing their plan, the group split up. Christina, Douglas, Nevills, and Black called a friend to drive them into a quiet neighborhood. Christina gave Nevills a gun and told him to find a victim and put them in the trunk of a car, then return to her trailer within an hour and a half.

Debra Cheeseborough was their first victim.

After the group thought they had killed Cheeseborough, they returned to Christina's trailer where they discussed their plan further. They realized that they needed another car. Christina, Tucker, Black, and Queen took Cheeseborough's car in search of another victim, ultimately finding Tracy Lambert and Susan Moore.

After killing the two young women, the group decided to call it a night and meet up at the trailer the next day. However, Tirado had trouble sleeping and kept one ear to the police scanner all night. At around dawn, he called Christina and reported to her that bodies had been found. From there, the entire group, with the exception of Black and Nevills, fled to Myrtle beach in Cheeseborough and Moore's cars, using her cell phone to place calls back to family and friends.

On Tuesday, August 18th, police in Myrtle Beach arrested Juarbe and Tucker and impounded Cheeseborough's car. The next day, they received an anonymous tip that Christina had rented a room at the Bona Villa motel in Myrtle Beach. They checked out the tip and found Moore's car in the parking lot. There, they apprehended Christina, Frink, Douglas, Queen, and Tirado. Soon, there was a media frenzy.

The Outcry

Throughout Fayetteville, the deaths of Lambert & Moore and the brutally savage attack on Debra Cheeseborough left the community enraged. The news that the crime spree was related to gang activity created a frenzy of individuals calling to "clean up the streets." News outlets flashed pictures of Moore and Lambert, two white, blonde haired, beautiful young ladies, but were less inclined to show images of Debra Cheeseborough, a middle-aged black woman. This, according to the defense, fed into a racial divide. Without knowing that Cheeseborough was a minority woman, herself, many within Fayetteville believed the violence was a hate crime against white people, instigated by a violent gang of minority youths. The fact that the attacks had been random was lost in the coverage and, soon, Fayetteville found itself in the throes of racial and economic divide.

The Woman

Not much is known about Christina's life before the events that unfolded that fateful night in 1998. Based on statements presented to her attorney, we can surmise that Christina's upbringing was less than ideal. She has made claims of being abused physically, emotionally, and sexually as a child. In one story, which would later come back to haunt her during trial, she spoke of cutting a man with a box cutter as he was trying to sexually abuse her.

As is the case with a lot of youths who feel displaced from their families and communities, Christina sought the embrace of whatever makeshift form of family she could find. In her case, she fell into a crowd of similarly dysfunctional minority youths who claimed membership to one of the largest street gangs in America: The Crips.

As Christina reached adulthood, she was able to secure her own place to live, which opened up a meeting ground for herself and fellow gang members to congregate in. Because her home was often the meeting point, she found herself in the position of leader and would often have to assert her dominance over other gang members who tried to challenge her. There is little doubt that the control Christina found within the gang was a welcome change from her helpless childhood. Christina no doubt realized that, in her newly given position, she could find safety in her power. She became a fearless leader of her group and was unafraid to assert herself with dominance or even threats of death.

Until that August night, though, Christina had never actually killed anyone. As would be explained in court by her co-defendants, to kill someone for the good of the gang is one of the highest honors the Crips had established at the time. The honor was memorialized with a teardrop tattoo on the face following a "confirmed kill."

Christina saw the carjacking plan as an opportunity to earn the highest honor she could for her gang, securing herself a position of leadership for life. To those of us who have grown up in more mild environments, it seems to be an act of selfishness and a fool's errand. To Christina, though, it would mean a lifetime of security from anyone that would ever attempt to cause her pain.

As the gang made plans to secure funds for their needs, Christina made plans of her own.

As the events unfolded, Christina remained mostly quiet about her intent to kill the carjacking victims. As each of the cars were stolen, the women were brought back to Christina's trailer to discuss their fates. It was only then that Christina expressed her desire for the women to be killed.

To refuse to kill someone for the benefit of the gang would have been suicide. With no other option but to help Christina, the co-defendants carried out Christina's plan alongside her. Because they had done so, Christina was responsible for helping them attempt to escape punishment, which is why she paid the way for everyone to go to Myrtle Beach.

Some of Christina's supporters today make a case that Christina wasn't cold-blooded. She was simply living the only life she knew how to survive in, and that her case was unnecessarily worsened by the media attention and dishonesty of news outlets at the time. Rumors regarding Christina's character and the lifestyle of the gang itself began to circulate. Soon enough, the story had evolved into a tale that Christina forced the co-defendants to kill two white women as a form of initiation into the gang. This was simply not the truth, but it was a tale that the defense had trouble running from. In the end, Christina "Shea" Walters believed the rumors and unfair media exposure were responsible for the severity of her sentencing.

The Trial

Regardless of Christina's culpability, she suffered from having inadequate representation at her trial. She was advised that, because of the media attention surrounding the case, the courts would issue a change of venue and try her somewhere other than Fayetteville. Unbeknownst to her, she would have had to file a motion for the change of venue. By the time she realized the need for her to initiate the motion, it was too late to file and her case was stuck at the center of a media whirlwind.

Because of the public nature of the case, Christina believes she was unable to receive a fair trial. According to her defense, eight of the twelve jurors that were seated on the jury had already been informed of the details of her case by other potential jurors and courtroom staff prior to the trial beginning. The state of North Carolina rebutted this claim stating that each juror swore to be fair and impartial and to disregard any information they had heard or read prior to the beginning of the proceedings. The state also argues that Christina never objected to the jurors at the appropriate time when she should have. Christina argues that, again, her defense team failed her and she did not know her rights.

She also claims she did not know her rights when she failed to file a motion for the murders of Lambert and Moore to be tried separately from the attack on Cheeseborough. Trying the crimes at the same time, she says, is partly to blame for the outcome of the proceedings.

Probably one of Christina's most compelling arguments that she did not receive a fair trial, however, comes with evidence logged right into the court report, itself. During the selection of the jurors, the Judge actually left the court room. During that time, a reporter began interviewing a potential juror about the case. The transcript reads as follows;

Judge: And, Madam Clerk, would you go ahead and call another juror please for number five?

Clerk: Richard Council.

Judge: Thank you. Counsel, I have to make a phone call to my district attorney. If you'll give me just a moment, please? (Leaves courtroom)

(Number five, Mr. Council, enters court room.)

Bailiff: Sir, come on up and have a seat in number five.

(A male media representative was talking to the juror, Mr. Council, as the juror walked by.)

Court Reporter: Tell that guy to quit talking to the juror- that media guy.

(Bailiff, Sgt. David Farrell, directed number five, Mr. Council, in the box after Sgt. Farrell spoke to the media representative.)

(Judge returns to courtroom.)

Judge: Remain seated.

Bailiff: Come to order. Court's in session.

Christina argues that, because the media had time to address the juror, and because nobody in the court room bothered to inform the Judge of the interaction, the juror was tampered with prior to the beginning of the proceedings and had already been given an "insider's idea" of what the hope of the community was for the outcome of her case.

Finally, Christina says that her past was brought up in court unnecessarily, with facts "twisted" to make her seem like a more brutal and violent person than she really believes herself to be. This is where the case falls back to the instance of self- defense against a sexual predator. Again, the evidence is in the transcript:

Prosecutor: Did you say your dad almost killed a boy that you stabbed?

Christina: I haven't stabbed no boy.

Prosecutor: Did you say that?

Christina: No, ma'am. I don't remember saying anything like that.

Prosecutor: Do you remember saying the boy you stabbed was 20-something at the time?

Christina: Unless the person who wrote this was talking about when I had a boyfriend who was trying to take my shirt off and I sliced him with a box cutter, but that's not stabbing.

At this point in the trial, the Judge did excuse the jury momentarily to ask the prosecutor why they were asking these questions. During the conversation, the Judge asked the defense why he had not objected to the questioning, clearly recognizing that it was a bad direction for the defense to allow the questioning to go.

Failing Christina, yet again, the defense attorney responded, "Well, because we didn't care at the point she was at."

One has to wonder- if a judge sees a line of questioning that is so outrageous he will dismiss the jury and ask, himself, why nobody is objecting to it- how does the defense, itself, not recognize the issue? Christina's supporters say that she was being defended by a court-appointed attorney who, they claim, was already swayed by the media outcry against Christina. He did not wish for her to win her case, so he did not even try to offer her a solid defense.

During the same testimony, Christina admitted that she shot several .32 caliber bullets into Cheeseborough, only stopping once she thought the victim was dead. Cheeseborough was able to testify against Walters, although she stated in her testimony that she could not positively identify her shooters. In appeals, Christina has stated that she was not well- advised by her attorney and only confessed to attempting to kill Cheeseborough because she believed that, because the victim of her shooting had survived, she would not be tied to the deaths of the other two women.

His failure to object to the unfair questioning, compiled with his failure to alert the judge of the jury tampering and not clearly outlining Christina's rights to her prior to trial are all signs indicating that, perhaps, Christina and her followers may be correct in their assumption.

In July of 2000, the trial came to a close with Christina Walters sentenced to Death. Eric Queen and Paco Tirado were both also sentenced to death in the months prior. With the ruling, Christina became the fifth woman on North Carolina's death row and secured herself a place as one of the state's most notorious female killers.

While there is little doubt that the acts committed against Tracy Lambert, Susan Moore, and Debra Cheeseborough on that August night were horrendous and cruel, there is reason to question whether or not Walters received a fair trial and sentencing in accordance with her legal rights under Federal law. Around the country, as news of the court case spread, Walters acquired supporters who felt empathy for her unfortunate upbringing and believed that she had been "railroaded" in court. As her following grew, the case began receiving attention from a new light, ultimately leading to a re-examination of the facts.

The Commuted Sentence

In December of 2012, a North Carolina judge commuted Christina Walters's death sentence along with the death sentences of two other convicted killers as part of the scaling back of the Racial Justice Act. The decision in each of the three cases came after a four-week deliberation on their individual cases in which the prosecution was proven to have made a conscious and indisputable error to reduce the number of black jurors in the original trials.

Although each of the prosecutors argued that they had, in fact, not made any such effort, the judge said that it was ultimately their own mannerisms and testimony that proved otherwise. "The conclusion is based primarily on the words and deeds of prosecutors involved in these cases," he said. "Despite presentations to the contrary, their words, their deeds, speak volumes. During presentation of evidence, the court finds powerful and persuasive evidence of racial consciousness, race-based decision making in the writings of prosecutors long buried in the case files and brought to light for the first time during this hearing."

Christina Walters, a Lumbee Indian, having been proven to have been tried unfairly based on her race, was commuted from death row to a life sentence without the possibility of parole.

The Repeal

In December of 2015, the Supreme Court vacated the commute claiming that the Judge did not give prosecutors adequate time to respond to a statistical study on race in the North Carolina state court system. The Racial Justice Act was also overturned, causing Christina Walters to, once again, have to appeal her case.

The study referenced concluded in 2011 showed that racial bias played a role in culling jurors before death penalty trials. Prosecutors disagreed with the claims, stating that the race of the juror doesn't play a role in their decision for keeping or releasing someone from the jury selection panel. The study examined 173 capital trials over a 20-year period to accumulate evidence to the contrary.

Qualified black jurors were over twice as likely to be released from panels under peremptory strikes according to Michigan State University's study of capital cases ranging from 1990 to 2010. Prosecutors argued that the study was invalid because the range of statistics stretched out far too broadly, failing to present an accurate depiction of how jurors are currently selected.

The Supreme Court encouraged both sides to prevent additional studies to support their claims.

In January of 2017, Christina Walters's legal team appealed her death sentence by using the now-repealed Racial Justice Act. Prosecutors argued that she couldn't use the repealed act because it has been repealed. Her defense argued that she had obtained relief under the Act and that it was unfair to strip her of that relief retroactively.

Judge Spainhour from Raleigh, North Carola presided over the case. He decided that Christina Walters's case was still pending under the Racial Justice Act and, therefore she could no longer use the repealed act.

There is little doubt that Christina Walters and her supporters will continue to appeal their case in pursuit of a commuted sentence or a retrial. With the buzz surrounding the case, it's hard not to look at the entirety of the situation objectively to determine if Christina is really the cold and calculated killer that prosecution in the original trial portrayed her to be or if, instead, she is a young woman led astray by circumstance, then railroaded by a court system designed to work against her.

Jay Ferguson, an attorney on her legal team, was quoted in the Fayetteville News Observer as saying, "We are confident that, no matter how many hearings are held or studies completed, we will win this case. The evidence of racial bias in jury selection is simply overwhelming and undeniable. All this decision will do is add more delays and cost the state millions to conduct new studies and hold new hearings. We will be throwing more taxpayer money into a hopelessly broken death penalty."

UGLY AS HELL: The True Story of Serial Killer Martha Wise

116

CARLA GLENN

*"The Devil made me do it," she said. "He came to me in my kitchen when I baked my bread and he said, 'Do it!' He came to me when I walked the fields in the cold days and nights and said, 'Do it!' Everywhere I turned I saw him grinning and pointing and talking. I couldn't eat. I couldn't sleep. I could only talk and listen to the devil. Then I did it!" - **Martha Wise**

Martha Wise was born in Hardscrabble, Ohio to parents who were farmers.

Her life fit the name of the town she was from, as she had to endure a harsh life of manual labor and insults from childhood up until her death.

When she entered school, her teachers immediately labeled her as "dull" and "stupid."

"She was the dumbest kid there," one of her teachers said while another recalled that Martha was "the dullest child in school. She was even too dull to make trouble."

Throughout Martha's childhood, she never met anyone who greeted her with kindness in the tough luck town of Hardscrabble. One of her classmates remembered Martha as "always crying and every time anyone spoke to her she would burst into tears."

With no friends or teachers on her side, Martha created her own little world of imaginary friends. She would have numerous playmates that were invisible only to her and have animated conversations with them.

Labeled "feeble minded" by her educators and a "moron" by the even less sympathetic neighbors, Martha's own parents held little hope for her future.

"A deep sense of self-pity, not at all unwarranted, grew in Martha," wrote Tom Sellers. "Just as she poisoned those who laughed. She learned to see the devil in every leering face she met."

Martha had three brothers and a sister but her family had little faith in her ability to leave the homestead and get married. Martha had deep set eyes that were spread wide across her face. Her putty nose, thin lips and broad cheekbones did little to flutter the hearts of eligible suitors.

"Let's face it," her own mother said to her sister Lillie. "Martha is ugly. Damn ugly."

In 1906, however, Martha would meet a man named Albert Wise at a box social. These box socials allowed eligible women to cook up a meal for bachelors in the area who would bid on their box. If they won the bid, they would be entitled to a date with the creator of the boxed meal.

"That was one helluva chicken sandwich," Albert Wise said as he chomped down on the meal that Martha had prepared for the box social. He was over twenty years her senior and not much to look at himself. Martha was in her early twenties but seemed destined for spinsterhood. She took to Albert's brief courtship all too willingly.

Albert would ask for Martha's hand in marriage and she happily obliged. He did not take the union seriously, however, as he didn't even give Martha a wedding ring.

"Let's go," Albert said after they exchanged vows. "There's work to be done."

Martha's dream of meeting and marrying Prince Charming soon came to a crashing halt as she arrived at Albert's fifty acre farm.

"Get to work bitch," Albert said as he threw a shovel at her. He then led Martha out to the pig sty where he forced her to clean up after the hogs.

Martha drew ridicule throughout the town of Hardscrabble as she was forced to do such harsh manual labor. The women in town worked hard but none of them were forced to slop the hogs.

Albert would work Martha like a rented mule. It became apparent that he married the homely young woman simply because he wanted a domestic slave.

"Hurry up!" Albert called out as Martha shoveled the pig feces into the compost pile. "After you're done, hoe the field and milk the cow. And then get your ass back inside and make me a chicken sandwich!"

Despite his advancing age and Martha's lack of appeal, Albert's sexual appetite was voracious. Martha would describe their sex life as "joyless" and "miserable." She would become pregnant but miscarry the baby because her farming duties were so strenuous. She and Albert would have four children, however; Everett, Gertrude, Kenneth and Lester.

Feeling nothing but self-pity, Martha developed an odd habit of attending funerals. She attended any funeral that was held in or near the town. She didn't care if she had known the deceased or not. When people asked what she was doing there she simply replied "I like funerals."

Martha's life on the farm continued to grow harsher as the money grew tight.

"Work, bitch, work!" Albert would cry out as he raked a hickory stick across Martha's buttocks and legs, imploring her to work harder around the farm. He would beat her as if she were a farm animal until one day Martha finally broke.

She would poison Albert in 1923 but would never be charged with the crime. The doctors performed no autopsy and chalked his death up to "stomach inflammation."

His death, however, had a silver lining for Martha as she was able to collect on his insurance policy. She obtained some freedom for the first time in her life and would often take long walks around the town, neglecting the farm work.

She also made sure that Albert had an elaborate funeral.

"There was music and there were flowers," Sellers wrote. "The children were clean and dressed in their best. And from nowhere, almost, there appeared the usual association of bearded ladies who hover about the homes where death has visited to offer consolation and solace. The stream of life suddenly lost some of its drabness."

Martha finally received some long sought after attention and sympathy during the funeral for her departed husband.

"I like funerals," she mumbled quietly to herself as the well-wishers slowly milled out of the graveyard.

Despite being free from the yoke of Albert, the now forty-year old Martha had four children to raise by herself. She continued indulging in her funeral fetish, attending services of strangers and making a spectacle of herself.

Martha would arrive at the funeral early and sit in the front row. She would cry and wail, screaming to the heavens, "Why! Why! Why!"

The theatrics would oftentimes scare other attendees while others would stare at Martha in open-mouthed shock.

"Dressed in her weeds, she attended all funerals within reach, her sobs and lamentations rising above the smothered tide of keening by the bereaved women," Sellers wrote. "Weeping became sheer joy to her. When the slightest thing went wrong she drew her children about her and sobbed, not the dry, choking sobs of the truly grief-stricken, but the free flood of tears that come easily to those afflicted with self-pity."

Despite being considered one of the ugliest and least desirable women in town, Martha decided to put herself back on the market for a new man.

Problem was that Martha was not a very attractive woman. She was now in her forties and had four young children. Friends and neighbors described her as a woman with a "pinched face and sunken eyes."

She would find a friend in Walter Johns, however, meeting the younger farmhand as he worked on a neighbor's property.

Martha would try her best to woo the man whenever she could. She would make him chicken sandwiches, bake fresh cookies and bring fresh lemonade to him on hot summer days when he worked out in the field. Johns was polite and appreciated the gestures but did not return the romantic interest.

Martha continued to try to win the man's heart through his stomach. Her actions soon brought ridicule from her neighbors and family members. They teased her mercilessly. Her own mother and aunt called her a "cradle snatcher" when they caught wind of the fact that she was trying to entice the younger man into an affair.

Both mother and aunt would take the bull by the horn and talk to Walter. They falsely accused Walter of having an affair with Martha which he vehemently denied. Disturbed by the accusations and rumors, Johns would move to Cleveland and would no longer see Martha.

Martha learned of his departure and was livid, blaming her family.

"Why can't you just let me have a little bit of happiness!" she cried out.

"You're old," her aunt said. "And ugly. It is for the best."

Martha, however, would begin to plot her revenge. The voices in her head, the ones from her childhood, being whispering louder in her ear.

"Do it," they wheezed.

"Do what?" she would ask aloud.

"Do it," the voices whispered again as she entered the drug store. She would purchase over fifty grams of arsenic which was supposed to be used only to kill rats.

"Do it," the voice in her head echoed, becoming louder.

Cradling the arsenic bottle, Martha knew what the voice in her head wanted her to do.

Martha would spike her family's kitchen water bucket with the rat poison. On Thanksgiving day of 1924, Martha would encourage all of the family members to drink up, excluding herself and her own children. Her mother Sophia, would fall ill as well as the rest of the visiting family.

"Arsenic poisoning is painful," Sellers wrote. "Imagine excruciating stomach pain for weeks on end. Your stomach is tied up in painful, tight knots and you can't stop vomiting and defecating."

Martha's mother, Sophia, would die after suffering for over three weeks. The rest of the family members would eventually recover.

Martha, however, would go all out for her mother's funeral, both in ceremony and performance.

"Why! Why! Why!" she wailed in the church pew as family members watched on in horror. She had to be helped in and out of her seat, her grief so severe.

She still had revenge on her mind, however. Her family had intervened and cost her the love of her life in Walter Johns.

They had to pay.

"Do it," the voice in her head repeated. "Do it."

Martha's face turned to stone as she knew her job was still incomplete. She still had a lot of left over arsenic remaining.

During the New Year's Eve celebration a few weeks after her mother's death, Martha once again spiked the family water bucket with arsenic.

This time, her uncle Fred and aunt Lillie Gienke were the victims along with their six children who ranged in age from nine to twenty-four.

Her aunt Lillie wold die on January 4th while the children and uncle Fred continued to have stomach cramps and uncontrolled bowel movements.

"It's bad," Fred said in describing his own violent battle with diarrhea. "Really bad."

The children would become hospitalized while Fred would lose his battle on February 8th, dying at the age of fifty-nine.

Their children were shipped off to neighbors and relatives. One of the children ended up in Martha's care.

Authorities, however, grew suspicious after the death of Uncle Fred. They initially thought the family were victims of botulism or other natural poisoning but that was not the case.

Sheriff Fred Roshon began looking into the activity of Martha and found out that she had purchased large quantities of arsenic at the local drug store. He decided to exhume the body of Martha's aunt Lillie and an autopsy revealed that she had, in fact, traces of arsenic in her stomach.

"But who could do this?" Roshon thought to himself. He brought in prosecutor Joseph Seymour and the two began to suspect Martha.

"Administration of the poison appears to have been accidental or the work of a moron," Seymour said to the press as they badgered him for answers on the rash of deaths.

Seymour would receive an anonymous letter in the mail, however. It read : "I just want to make a suggestion-see if you can find out if there was ill feeling between Martha Wise and Lillie Gienke. I know something of the treachery of this Martha Hasel Wise and also her craftiness to evade suspicion. She is what you might call a moron. Could it be to get rid of her mother and get the property and of Lillie of suspecting her. She claimed to have been made sick too, but that may be a lie too."

Seymour informed the Sheriff of the letter and the men brought in Martha for questioning.

"My heart bleeds for them (her dead family members)," Martha said as she entered the interrogation room. "It must have been a monster that would kill them, and my poor, innocent old mother, why did they kill her? It was terrible. I sometimes think they were poisoned by accident. Because I can't imagine anyone being so terrible."

Sheriff Roshon was joined in the room by his wife Ethel and Seymour.

"We know you did it, Martha," the Sheriff said, sitting across from her.

Martha said nothing. She gulped hard and looked at the Sheriff's wife for help.

"Why not confess and get it off your conscience?" Seymour said.

"You're wrong, Mr. Seymour," Martha said. "I would never a done such a thing."

"Why did you buy all of that arsenic?" Roshon asked.

"To kill some rats," Martha said, shifting in her seat.

"Rats?"

"Yeah."

"You purchased enough arsenic to kill all of the rats in the whole state! You did it to kill your family! Admit it!"

"No," Martha shook her head violently. Her eyes began to water.

"Martha, we found arsenic in your aunt Lily's stomach," the sheriff explained, holding up a receipt of her purchase of the rat poison. "We know how you warned your own kids not to drink water at grandma's or Uncle Fred's."

Tears streamed down Martha's face. Her bottom lip began to quiver.

The sheriff stared at the woman, letting several minutes pass. It began to rain outside.

Ethel Roshon, the sheriff's wife, then took Martha's hand.

"Listen, Martha," Ethel said. "Do you hear those raindrops? Do you hear what they're saying? They're saying: 'Drop-drip-drip. You-did-it. Drop-drip-drip. You-did-it.' You did it, Martha! You know you did! Listen to it, Martha. It's the voice of God. He's telling you to tell the truth!"

"Oh, my God!" Martha screamed. "Yes, I did it. I put arsenic in the water bucket. But it was the Devil that told me to. He came to me, laughing and grinning, while I baked my bread. He came to me when I was a-hoin' in the fields. He kept telling me to do it while he follered me in the meadow. It was the Devil done it."

"The devil?" the sheriff asked.

"They told me I had no business wantin' to get married again. Said I was old and ugly. They laughed at me when that young fellow threw me over. I hated them and the Devil said: 'Kill them!' And I did. I liked their funerals. I could get dressed up and see folks and talk to them. I didn't miss a funeral in twenty years. The only fun I ever had was after I kilt people."

The sheriff got up out of his seat, aghast. "Why, Martha? Why would you do such a thing?"

"I'm irresistibly attracted to attending funerals," Martha said. "We do not have enough funerals here. I had to create them myself. I'm sure you understand."

The trio sat in silence, letting the weight of the confession sink in.

"I did it all," Martha said. "I stole jewelry from friends. Family. The barns that burned down? That was me. I like fires. They were red and bright, and I loved to see the flames shooting up into the sky."

Sheriff Roshon never made the connection between Martha and the three churches that had been set on fire in the town. He now had his perpetrator that he would have never suspected.

The prosecution attorney met with doctors and they all determined that Martha was suffering from "mental dementia." Despite the diagnosis and facing pressure from both the newspaper and local townspeople, Seymour decided to prosecute Martha to the full extent of the law.

The trial was set for May 4th, 1925.

Wise would plead not guilty despite the fact that she confessed during the police interrogation.

The press and local townspeople had a field day with daily news reports and gossip. Martha would be described as the "Borgia of America," a reference to the crime family that specialized in arsenic poisoning.

The press had built her up as a monster, printing unflattering pictures of her and then describing her as a 'super-killer' when she went into the courtroom. One newspaper wrote "her face was drawn, her eyes downcast. There were lines about her eyes and mouth, testifying to the mental suffering thru which she has passed during the months that she has been in jail. Her hair was combed straight back from her wrinkled and yellow forehead. Her eyes were weird, dark caverns, deep-sunk behind her steel-rimmed glasses. When she was arrested her hair showed few traces of gray. Today it is thickly streaked with white...The woman walked like one very tired. Her shoulders sagged. Her head dropped on a sunken chest. Her clothes were clean, but ill-fitting over her gaunt form. Her hands hung listlessly at her sides, one clutching, claw-like, a small-blue handkerchief."

Martha was assigned an attorney named Joseph Pritchard who would prove to be just as moronic as Martha herself, a match made in hell. His initial argument to the grand jury was that Martha was insane and should not have to go to trial. The jury refused and Pritchard then had to come up with new ploys. He planned to foist the blame on Martha's sister-in-law, Edith.

Edith had been troubled by delusions that she was the one that had poisoned the Gienke and Hasel families. She became frightened that Pritchard would call her to the stand as voices in her head told her that she did it. When authorities informed her that Pritchard was going to force her to testify, Edith slashed her own throat with a paring knife. Martha's brother Fred then had a heart attack upon hearing of his wife's suicide. So instead of taking the stand to defend his sister, he was in the hospital.

Pritchard knew he was working against a stacked deck. Martha's own son Lester and three of Gienke's children would testify against the prosecution. Lester would inform the jury that his mother gave him distinct instructions not to drink the water during the Holiday parties.

Martha's nieces and nephews would hobble into the courtroom on crutches and struggle to take the stand. The prosecution made them describe their daily lives, giving detailed accounts on what it was now like to be partially paralyzed due to the arsenic poisoning administered by Martha.

Pritchard scratched his head for a new tactic. He convinced the authorities that Martha's love interest, Walter Johns, had put her up to killing the families as he was upset that he was forced to move to Cleveland.

Johns was then arrested and held in jail for a few days.

The press and local townspeople had a field day with the revelation. The townsfolk started rumors about Johns having an affair with Martha. They made jokes that the crazy Martha would be on all fours during their lovemaking sessions, barking like a dog as she experienced an orgasm.

Pritchard then called Martha to the stand and had her recount the time spent with Walter Johns.

"I would have carried this to the grave," Martha said. "I never intended to tell. But now that everybody is talking about it, I can't hold my tongue any longer. He never came to see me in the jail and at the trial he never looked at me, although he was there every day. Walter Johns told me to do it. It wasn't the devil-it was Walter Johns. They didn't want me to get married. He said to get Mother out of the way and I did. He made me do it! He put me up to it! He kept at me to do it! He told me I should get the arsenic and get rid of my mother, and then I'd be free and happy...I took my punishment. You scorned me. Now I tell."

"She lies," Johns said. "She lies. I don't know anything about this."

A police investigation would prove that Johns was an innocent man who was merely being nice to Martha. He was a married man with five children. A hard worker of whom no one had anything bad to say about.

"We were never lovers," Johns said, shaking his head after he was released from jail.

Pritchard was then forced to come up with something new in Martha's defense.

The man's name was Frank Metzger.

Pritchard had used this technique numerous times in his career. He would pay off a fake witness who would come forward and say what needed to be said in order to get his client off the hook.

"I call Frank Metzger to the stand," Pritchard said.

They watched as the small time criminal walked toward the stand.

"This man's story will save you," Pritchard whispered into Martha's ear.

"I know nothing of about the case," Metzger said as Pritchard began questioning him.

"What?"

"I never spoke to Mrs. Wise. I never saw Mrs. Wise. Ever."

Pritchard turned red. He had paid off Metzger but now the man reneged on his end of the bargain. The case was the talk of the whole country and Metzger sensed that there would be repercussions if he was caught perjuring himself.

Pritchard now had no choice but to allow the prosecution to question the man.

"The defense wanted me to perjure myself," Metzger said to a stunned jury. "I asked asked to have written out a statement that Martha Wise was, inside and that I saw her froth at the mouth and heard her bark like a dog. I never saw or heard any such thing."

Pritchard's trump card now coming to naught, he resorted to crocodile tears during his own closing arguments. He described Martha's wretched life in vivid detail and in closing focused on her mental illness.

"Pyromania, plus kleptomania, plus epilepsy, plus spinal meningitis equals insanity," Pritchard said as he returned to his seat.

"This is no town lunatic," prosecuting attorney Seymour said as he closed his own argument. "This is a cunning and sly murderer. Imagine her slipping into the Gienke home when no one was watching, pinching arsenic into their water pail, returning twice to add further poison-that's not the manner in which insane people kill. She bought enough arsenic to kill every one in the Hardscrabble district where she lived. She came to the Gienkes when they all were ill and told their doctor she thought their illness was influenza. That's not the act of an insane woman."

The jury would deliberate for less than an hour. Martha would be found guilty of first-degree murder but the jury suggested mercy in her sentencing.

The judge would sentence Martha to a life sentence under terms in which she could only be freed by executive clemency. At the time, it was highly doubtful that this clemency would ever occur.

"The devil made me do it," Martha said after her conviction. "Voices told me to. After I did it, it bothered me and worried me. I worried about it all the time. I feel better now...I feel better since I have told you all about it...It is the Lord's will that I should be punished and I know I must be."

Martha's children, Lester 14, Everett 11, Gertrude 10 and Kenneth, 7 were all placed into adopted homes. Martha's netw worth was worth only the eighteen-acre farm and $1800 in savings.

Martha would remain in the public eye, her crimes would become the stuff of legend in the Hardscrabble community. A news reporter would visit her in 1930, five years after her conviction.

Martha would express remorse in the interview and continue to describe encounters with the supernatural.

"I see ghosts," she said to the reporter. "Every night they come and sit on the edge of my bed in their grave clothes. They point their fingers at me."

Jail life would be a routine for Martha. She would take two baths a week. She would get up at 6 a.m. and have the lights turned off in her room by 8 p.m.

"I do what I am told to do," she said in describing her prison life. Her duties were similar to what she did on the farm. She fed the chickens and played with the rabbits. She found happiness in incarceration but would cry when reminded of her children.

She would be denied parole in 1946, 1951, and 1956 but finally got a break on December 26th, 1962.

After almost three decades in prison, Ohio Governor Michael DiSalle would commute Martha's sentence to second-degree murder. She would be paroled at age 79 but would have nowhere to go. Her family refused to take her in and the correctional institute could not find a rest home who would accept her. Initially, she was going to be placed in a rest home in Union county where the prison was located. She would fail the one-year residency requirement, however. Officials then made arrangements through a senior citizen center run by Murial Worthing.

Worthing had initially agreed to take in the elderly killer but reneged after discovering her personal history.

"No," Worthing said. "She cannot come into our house. I'm a food caterer. This is a small town. People would talk. What do you think would happen to my business? I'd even lose the job as a cook I'm now holding."

"After I did it, it bothered me and worried me," Martha said. "I worried about it all the time. I feel better now...I feel better since I have told you all about it...It is the Lord's will that I should be punished and I know I must be."

Martha's probation officer had no choice but to take her in for the night. The next morning, she drove her back to the jail as Martha wept.

"There was no reason why this woman should have ever left the reformatory," Governor DiSalle said after the plans for her to go to the Union county home fell through. "This casts a reflection on state workers up and down the line because somebody didn't do the job."

Her parole and commutation of her sentence was revoked simply because there was no where for her to go.

Martha was then forced to live her remaining years in the Marysville reformatory for women.

Martha Wise, the woman no one wanted, would die in prison on June 28th, 1971 at the age of 88.

www.ingramcontent.com/pod-product-compliance
Lightning Source LLC
Chambersburg PA
CBHW030335160726
47987CB00021B/636

"Este copleșitoare povestea adopției lui Ionuț dintr-un orfelinat din România de către familia Kuhls, pentru mine, ca român care a avut șansa să îl întâlnească pe Ionuț pentru prima dată în casa familiei Barb și Ron. Faptul că ei au ales să adopte un copil cu cele mai mari nevoi arată nivelul profund de iubire pe care Dumnezeu l-a așezat în inima celor doi soți. Ani mai târziu, privind la reuniunea lui Ionuț cu familia sa biologică la Huși, în România, văd ca pe o minune a lui Dumnezeu în care Și-a manifestat harul din belșug."

— **Mihai Dumitrașcu**,
Pastor Senior, Biserica Emanuel, Galați, România

"În calitate de pastor al bisericii frecventate de familia Kuhls, am fost martor direct al poveștii relatate în această carte. Poate te întrebi dacă Dumnezeu vorbește vreodată în ziua de azi. Poate te întrebi dacă Dumnezeu este în stare să facă vindecări adevărate și transformare minunată. Povestea lui Noot este un miracol și un răspuns în carne și oase la întrebarea despre implicarea lui Dumnezeu din ziua de azi.

Îmi amintesc prima dată când l-am văzut pe Noot mergând/alergând pe holurile bisericii la scurt timp după ce a sosit în SUA (înainte să i se monteze protezele la picioare). Era plin de energie, o personalitate molipsitoare și de un optimism de neoprit. Având eu însumi un copil adoptat dintr-o altă cultură, înțeleg pe deplin îngrijorările și temerile oricărui părinte adoptiv care face pasul adopției transculturale. Ron și Barb sunt exemple extraordinare ale adopțiilor inspirate de Dumnezeu. Mai mult decât atât, povestea nu s-a terminat. Noot continuă să scrie noi capitole de-a lungul propriei sale călătorii de credință și implicare. Vă mulțumesc că ne-ați împărtășit povestea voastră, și vă mulțumesc că sunteți un exemplu viu de credință simplă și curajoasă."

—**Ken Nabi**, Președinte Regional Converge Great Lakes

"În această poveste extraordinară despre adopție, visul incredibil al unei femei se transformă într-o realitate incredibilă. De la început până la uluitorul sfârșit sunt vizibile amprentele lui Dumnezeu. Cititorul va reieși inspirat pe deplin de un copil care a început viața având un viitor incert și care acum zboară ca vulturii."

—**Kristi Wilkinson**, Autor, *The Child Who Listens*